Anchored in the Weeds

Walking Every Eternal Destination—Surrounded

Delia L. Mitchell

Disclaimer:

This publication is provided for inspirational and informational purposes only. It is not intended as medical, psychological, or professional counseling advice. The author and publisher disclaim any liability arising directly or indirectly from the use or application of the information contained in this book. Readers are encouraged to seek professional guidance where appropriate.

Publisher:

Jacinth Media Productions LLC

Allentown, PA

info@JacinthMediaProductions.com

www.JacinthMediaProductions.com

ISBNs:

Paperback: 978-1-960594-53-2

Hardback: 978-1-960594-54-9

eBook: 978-1-960594-55-6

Library of Congress Control Number: 2026907162

First Edition: 2026

Printed in the United States of America

Contents

Anchored in the Weeds

In this journey, **WEEDS** are not obstacles to remove.
They are a reminder of how faith grows even when it cannot be seen.

W — ***Walking*** — Faith is not static. Walking honors process. It allows questions, pauses, and progress without perfection.

E — ***Every*** — God is present in every step, every season, every emotion, every stage of becoming.

E — ***Eternal*** — Our journey is shaped by more than immediate outcomes. What we practice now is forming us for what lasts.

D — ***Destination*** — A destination is not always a place—it is a direction. God's destinations are often revealed while walking, not before starting. The journey itself becomes part of God's purpose.

S — ***Surrounded and Rooted in Grace*** — Grace often grows beneath the surface—unnoticed, unnamed, uncelebrated. Just like roots beneath the soil, grace is working even when we don't feel it.

— Delia L. Mitchell

Dedication

Anchored in the Weeds is dedicated to **my daughters**, **Terry**—the artist behind this book's cover—and **Ryan**, who continually challenge me and teach me the true meaning of being anchored. Through them, I have learned strength, hope, and the courage to remain rooted even as I grow.

To **my mother**, **Deborah**, who has shown me what grace looks like in practice and what strength looks like when it is lived with humility.

To **my sister, Tylisha Mitchell**, for her hard work and brilliant creativity—your excellence and steady support have been a gift to this journey.

To **my nieces**, whose unfolding futures remind me why legacy matters and why faith must be lived boldly and truthfully.

To **my aunts, brothers, cousins, uncles,** and to **every woman** who has called me higher, held space for my becoming, and reminded me who I am when the way forward felt unclear.

And to the **youth** who have allowed me the honor of discipleship—
who have trusted me with their questions, their searching, and their growth.
You continue to teach me
as much as I seek to teach you.
This journey is ours.
I remain anchored because of you.

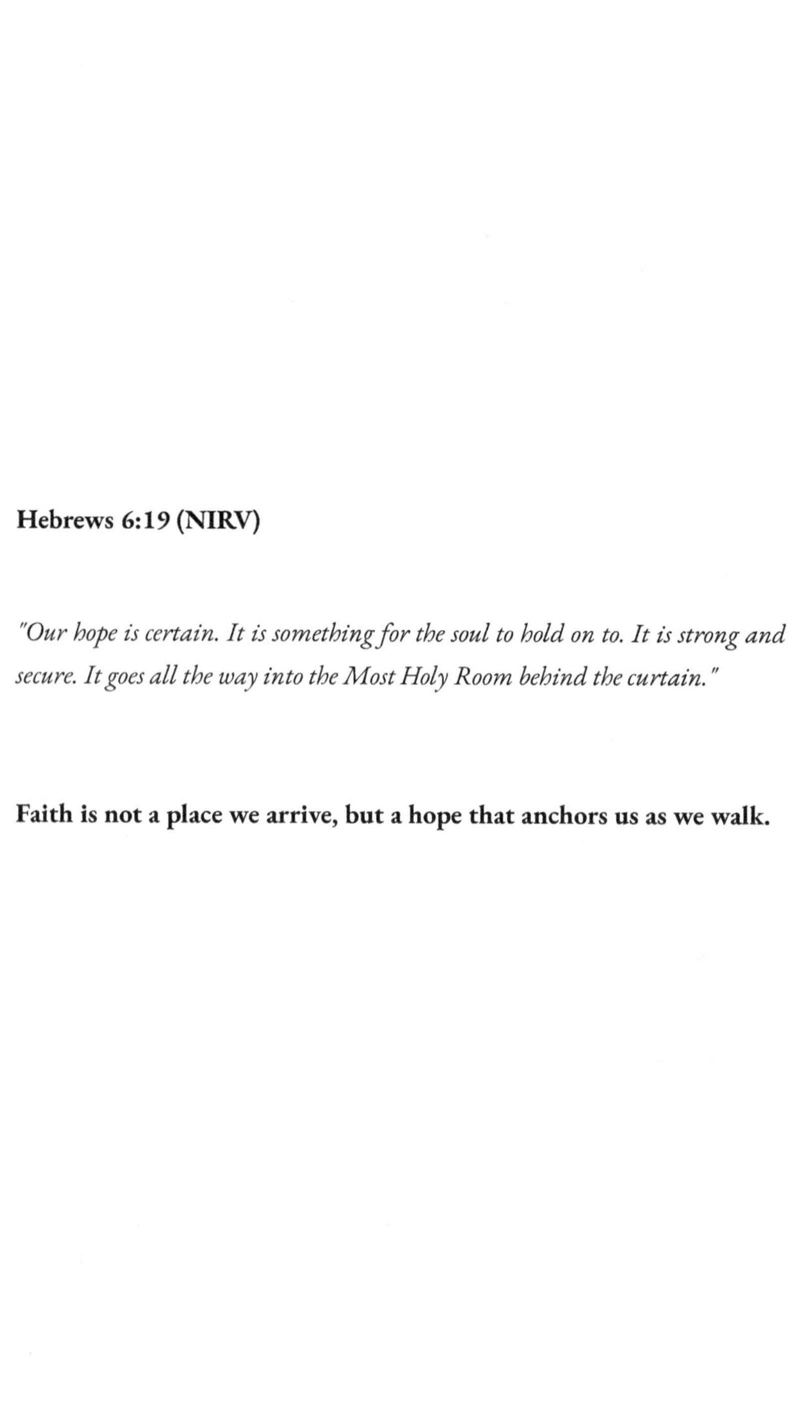

Hebrews 6:19 (NIRV)

"Our hope is certain. It is something for the soul to hold on to. It is strong and secure. It goes all the way into the Most Holy Room behind the curtain."

Faith is not a place we arrive, but a hope that anchors us as we walk.

Introduction

ANCHORED IN THE WEEDS

In 2020, during the height of the COVID-19 pandemic, I was introduced to Dr. Celeste C. Owens, MD—may she rest in eternal power. She led a 40-day Surrender Fast at a time when the world was marked by global crisis, racial unrest, grief, and deep uncertainty.

In that season, I longed to hear from God more clearly. Through a sister-friend, I joined the fast—yes, fasting during COVID. When so much had already been stripped away, I chose to surrender more—not from obligation, but from desire.

Psalm 42:1 (NIV)

"As the deer pants for streams of water, so my soul pants for you, my God."

That verse reflected the posture of my heart. Through daily prayer, Scripture, and community, I was renewed. During those forty days, I accepted my calling into preaching and teaching ministry and completed my Biblical Counseling certification.

That experience remained with me.

Two years later, I felt led to guide the women of my church through a 28-day fast and prayer journey. The number twenty-eight was intentional—four cycles of seven. Seven represents completion and divine order; four reflects the fullness of creation. Together, they symbolize faith lived out in everyday life.

The first fast began in September 2023. Women joined me in preparing weeks of Scripture, prayer, and song. By 2025, I was strengthened to lead the full 28-day journey and gather three years of devotionals—over sixty reflections that guided women into fellowship and formation.

The testimonies were powerful:
"I was blessed every day and didn't want it to end."
"I received revelation during prayer and fasting."
"The community encouraged me."
"The Holy Spirit led me to start my business."

Through it all, I have seen that being strengthened by the true Source—Jesus Christ—anchors us through life's most challenging seasons.

While preparing a Bible study as a minister-in-training, God gave me the phrase:
Walking Every Eternal Destination—Surrounded by unseen grace, unspoken prayers, and a God who walks with us.

In time, I understood: God was not only walking with me—He was anchoring me. My prayer is that this 28-day journey reminds you that you do not walk alone. There is an anchor—even in the weeds.

Numbers 6:24-26 (NIRV)
*"May the Lord bless you and keep you.
May His face shine upon you and give you peace."*

With you on the journey,

Delia Mitchell
Mother • Author • Biblical Teacher

A Scripture Companion for Prayer and Fasting

Begin this journey not striving for perfection, but surrendering with intention.

This 28-day companion is grounded in Scripture—not as an obligation, but as an invitation into deeper communion with God. The Word does not simply accompany the fast; it sustains it. Scripture becomes our anchor when hunger exposes weakness, our compass when emotions rise, and our steady voice when distractions press in.

Fasting without the Word can become discipline without direction. But when fasting is joined with Scripture, our focus shifts from what we are relinquishing to whom we are drawing near. We remember that fasting is not self-denial for its own sake—it is spiritual alignment. As Jesus reminds us, "People do not live by bread alone, but by every word that comes from the mouth of God" (Matthew 4:4 NLT).

Each day's passage is meant to be read slowly, prayed through honestly, and carried into daily living. The accompanying song selections are invitations into worship, allowing truth to move from the mind into the heart. Whether you are new to fasting or continuing a long-standing practice, this rhythm creates sacred space for reflection, repentance, renewal, and revelation.

Through Scripture and prayer, we learn to listen more closely, respond more faithfully, and trust more deeply. And in doing so, we discover that even in the weeds—God is forming something steadfast within us.

Week 1: Anchored in Renewal

REMEMBERING GOD'S WORKS —TRUSTING THE PROCESS

Day 1

TRUSTING GOD WITH YOUR TRANSFORMATION

Anchored in the Morning

Anchoring Scripture

Psalm 111:4-6 (NIRV)

"The Lord causes his wonders to be remembered. He is kind and tender. He provides food for those who have respect for him. He remembers his covenant forever. He has shown his people what his power can do. He has given them the lands of other nations."

Anchoring Thought

Psalm 111 speaks to a foundational truth: the Lord is indeed gracious. He is a God who sends redemption to His people, and all that He does is honorable and worthy of praise. As we walk through this process of transformation, we can rest assured that the same God who began a good work in us will faithfully complete it until the work is done. Therefore, we can trust God with our transformation. As He reshapes us into the *Imago Dei*—His very image—we respond with wholehearted praise, confident that when God is finished with us, we will come forth as pure gold.

Anchoring Prayer

Our Father, God Almighty, gracious and merciful Lord,
We come to You with grateful hearts, thanking You for Your plan and purpose for our lives. Thank You for loving us enough to guide our steps and work all things together so that we may become whole in You.
As we step into this season, we surrender ourselves to You and trust You with our transformation. Help us stay steady and focused on what matters, even when growth feels uncomfortable. Open our hearts and purify us, shaping us into who You created us to be. We thank You in advance for doing what we cannot do on our own—for giving us new vision, deeper understanding, and faith to keep going. We choose to praise You with our whole hearts, trusting that as You work in us, we will come out stronger, wiser, and refined.
We pray this in Jesus' name, Amen.

Song of Praise | Yahweh (Live) - Transformation Worship

Anchored at Night

Trusting God's Provision

Anchoring Scripture

Psalm 119:33 (NIRV)

"Lord, teach me how your orders direct me to live. Then I will live that way to the very end."

Anchoring Thought

Psalm 119:105 reminds us that God's Word is a lamp for our feet and a light for our path. It does not always show the entire journey, but it gives enough light to walk faithfully—one step at a time. Through His Word, God reveals truth, direction, and purpose.

When we repent and submit to God's will, we place ourselves in alignment with His guidance. Surrender is not weakness; it is trust. As we yield our hearts to Him, God faithfully directs our steps and leads us in the way we should go. Our God is faithful to do exactly what He says. What He promises, He performs. As this day ends, we rest knowing that we are not walking alone—we are being led by the light of His Word. We are anchored, even at night.

Night Prayer

Lord, as I settle into rest, I meditate on Your Word and reflect on Your goodness. I surrender fully to Your transforming work, trusting that You know what is best for me and that You provide according to Your will and Your riches in glory. Have Your way in my life. Forgive me for the moments when I have moved ahead of You instead of waiting on You. Thank You for carrying me through this day and for the work You continue to do within me, even as I sleep. I rest in Your peace and place my trust in You. I trust You, God, with everything I cannot

carry into tomorrow.
In Jesus' name, Amen.

Song of Praise | Teach Me Oh Lord - Vanessa Bell Armstrong

Anchoring Reflections
Day 1

1.Noticing God Today

Psalm 111 reminds us that God wants us to remember what He does, and Psalm 119 encourages us to keep His Word close to our hearts. Where did you see or feel God at work today, and how did something you read, heard, or remembered from Scripture help guide you?

2. Learning to Trust God

God promises to care for those who honor Him, and His Word teaches us how to walk in His ways. What did God provide for you today—help, patience, courage, peace—and was there a moment when you had to choose to trust Him instead of doing things your own way?

3. Growing and Becoming

God keeps His promises and uses His Word to shape who we are. How did today stretch you or help you grow, and what is one way God is helping you become more like the person He created you to be?

Day 2

MAKE ROOM

Anchored in the Morning

Anchoring Scripture

Luke 6:46-48 (NIRV)

"Why do you call me, 'Lord, Lord,' and still don't do what I say? Some people come and listen to me and do what I say. I will show you what they are like. They are like a man who builds a house. He digs down deep and sets it on solid rock. When a flood comes, the river rushes against the house. But the water can't shake it. The house is well built."

Anchoring Thought

The Gospel of Luke presents the life and teachings of Jesus Christ with careful detail, emphasizing not only what Jesus said, but how His words call for transformed living. In Luke 6:46–48, Jesus challenges those who call Him "Lord" yet refuse to live according to His instruction.

Jesus exposes a tension that existed among the Pharisees—and still exists today: honoring God with words while clinging to personal opinions, traditions, and self-directed ways of living. They heard Jesus' teaching, but resisted surrender. They wanted authority without obedience. In this passage, Jesus calls all who follow Him to build their lives on a solid foundation. Building on the rock requires humility—getting out of our own way, releasing control over our thoughts and actions, and making room for God's truth to lead us. This is not passive belief; it is active obedience.

To build on the rock is to surrender fully—to follow Christ in spirit and in truth, trusting His way above our own. Obedience prepares the foundation. Surrender strengthens the structure. And a life anchored in Christ cannot be shaken when the storms come. A house built on solid rock will stand firm. It will not collapse under pressure. It will not be washed away by rising tides.

Anchoring Prayer

Mighty God, thank You for another day of Your grace and mercy. In a turbulent world, You remain our living hope—the keeper of our souls and the One we praise with our whole hearts.

Search us, Lord, and reveal the places where we have not surrendered or walked in obedience. Your Word teaches us that obedience is better than sacrifice. Help us not to hear Your Word without action, but to walk in trust—moving when You say move and waiting when You say wait.

Thank You for seeing our weaknesses and blessing us beyond them. Go before us and lead us in paths of righteousness. We trust Your power at work in our lives

and believe You will do what You have promised.
In Jesus' name, Amen.

Song of Praise | Make Room - Jonathan McReynolds

Anchored at Night

Saved to Surrender

Anchoring Scripture

Galatians 2:20 (NIRV)

"I have been crucified with Christ. I don't live any longer, but Christ lives in me. Now I live my life in my body by faith in the Son of God. He loved me and gave himself for me."

Anchoring Thought

In Galatians, Paul speaks to believers who were struggling to understand their identity and their purpose in Christ. They were being pulled between old ways of living and the new life offered through faith. Paul reminds them—and us—that when we accept Christ, our lives are no longer our own.

To be saved is to enter a surrendered life. We do not live by our own strength, wisdom, or direction anymore. Christ lives in us, and we now look to Him for truth, light, and guidance. This surrendered life does not remove hardship, but it gives meaning to our suffering and clarity to our calling.

Even in moments of weakness or uncertainty, surrender anchors us. When Christ lives in us, we walk in our true identity—not shaped by fear or pressure but formed by faith. This is the way of life fully given to Him.

Night Prayer

Tonight, I rest knowing my life belongs to Christ and is held securely in Him. Almighty God, I thank You for Your lavish grace, tender mercy, and unfailing love. I stand in awe of You and delight myself in You. Thank You for placing within me the desire to surrender—to die to self and live fully for You.

Remove anything in me that does not align with Your Holy Spirit. I believe You created me as an image-bearer, called to walk in the authority and purpose You have given me. Surrender is my walk of faith, and today I submit myself to You—Your will over my own, Your mission over my agenda.

I thank You in advance for the transformation You are bringing in my life. In Jesus' name, Amen.

Song of Praise | I Surrender - Tasha Cobbs Leonard

Anchoring Reflections

Day 2

1.Surrender

What do I need to release tonight and trust God with?

2. Identity

Where am I anchoring my identity—in Christ or in my performance or past?

3. Trust

What is the next faithful step God is inviting me to take?

4. Rest

What would it look like to truly rest, trusting that God is still working?

5. Making Room

"Galatians 2:20 says it is no longer you who lives, but Christ who lives in you. What is one thing — a habit, a worry, a version of yourself — that you sense God asking you to release in order to make room for more of Him today?"

Day 3

Unrooted Pressure

Anchored in the Morning

Anchoring Scripture

2 Corinthians 13:5-6 (NIRV)

"Take a good look at yourselves to see if you are really believers. Test yourselves. Don't you realize that Christ Jesus is in you? Unless, of course, you fail the test! I hope you will discover that I haven't failed the test."

Anchoring Thought

It is easy to place pressure on ourselves—pressure from the world to show up in ways that are not aligned with who we truly are. Over time, this pressure creates inner turmoil that leads to stress, guilt, and confusion.

In his letter to the church at Corinth, Paul calls believers to examine themselves—to test whether they are living according to the ways of the world or truly living in Christ Jesus. This invitation is not meant to shame, but to bring clarity and alignment.

Living for Christ means uprooting pressure that does not come from Him. It requires a spiritual check-up rooted in Christ—one that anchors the heart in surrender and obedience and leads us back to the one true and living God. When we uproot pressure that comes from ourselves—pressure that leads to guilt and condemnation—and instead root our lives in Christ, transformation begins. A renewed mind, a pure heart, and clean hands are the fruit of a life anchored in Him.

Anchoring Prayer

Dear Lord, Heavenly Father, I come to You thanking You for Your deep love and for working all things together for my good. I seek You with my whole heart and ask that You would purify my heart, allowing Your living water to flow through me. Guard my heart and mind. Uproot anything in me that does not align with You, so that I am not conformed to this world, but transformed by the renewing of my mind. During this time of fasting and prayer, form my heart posture and shape me according to Your will. I yield to the work You desire to do in me. Let the transformation that begins in my heart flow into my home, my relationships, my community, and every place You have called me. Help me to steward my time with You through prayer, meditation, and Your Word.

I thank You in advance for the holy work You are doing in me right now. I give You all the glory and trust that Your will is being accomplished. In Jesus' name, Amen.

Song of Praise | Give Me A Clean Heart - Jordan G. Welch

Anchored at Night

A Surrendered Heart

Anchoring Scripture

Jeremiah 24:7 (NIRV)
"I will change their hearts. Then they will know that I am the Lord. They will be my people, and I will be their God. They will return to me with all their hearts."

Anchoring Thought

Scripture reminds us that the heart, on its own, cannot be trusted. As the prophet Jeremiah teaches, the heart can be deceptive and easily led by fear, pride, or self-will. It is only through surrender to God that our hearts are made right.

A surrendered heart allows God to do the transforming work we cannot do ourselves. When we yield our will to Him, our hearts are realigned, renewed, and shaped according to His purpose. From that place of surrender, our steps become ordered and our lives come into alignment with God's will.

True peace and direction flow from a heart fully given to God. Surrender is not loss—it is the pathway to becoming who God has called us to be.

Night Prayer

Tonight, I rest knowing God is shaping my heart as I surrender fully to Him. Dear Lord, thank You for the grace You give me and for the invitation to surrender my whole heart to You. I place my heart in Your hands—transform me into Your likeness and shape me according to Your will.

Let every desire within me come from a heart that has fully returned to You.

Have Your way in my life and let Your will be done.

In Jesus' name, Amen.

Song of Praise | YES - Harmony Dobson

Anchoring Reflections

Day 3

1.Heart Check-Up

What is shaping my heart right now—fear, expectations, or trust in God?

2. Prayer

How is God inviting me to trust Him more deeply?

What do I need to place in God's hands before I rest tonight?

3. Spiritual Check-Up

What has been draining me that God never asked me to carry?

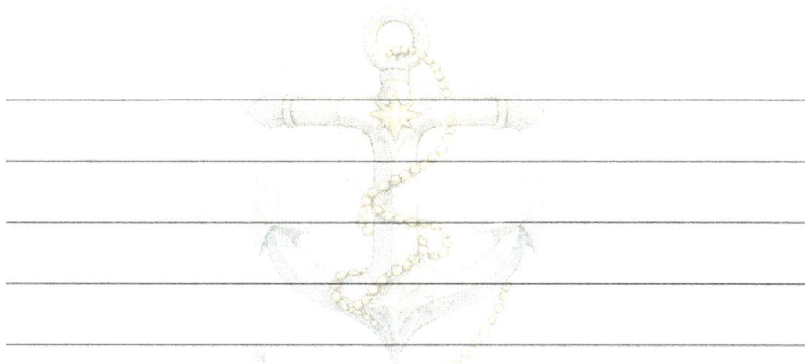

4. Becoming

2 Corinthians 13:5 invites you to look honestly at yourself and discover Christ already living in you. As you surrender the pressure you were never meant to carry, what do you sense God is forming in you — and what would it look like to walk in that version of yourself tomorrow?

Day 4

UNDIVIDED ATTENTION

Anchored in the Morning

Anchoring Scripture

Matthew 5:6 (NIRV)

"Blessed are those who are hungry and thirsty for what is right. They will be filled."

Anchoring Thought

In Matthew 5, Jesus shares the Beatitudes with the crowd that gathered to hear Him teach. Many in the crowd were physically hungry, having traveled a long distance just to be near Him. Yet Jesus points beyond physical hunger to something deeper—a hunger for righteousness and for the true and living God.

Jesus teaches that blessing comes not from having everything figured out, but from desiring what is right and aligning our hearts with God. To hunger and thirst for righteousness is to give God our undivided attention—to want His way, His truth, and His presence more than anything else.

Matthew reminds us that when we seek God with sincere desire and long to live in right relationship with Him, He promises to fill us. This filling is daily, sustainable, and sufficient for the journey. When our attention is focused on God, our hearts are satisfied.

Anchoring Prayer

Father, I pray that in this season I remain rooted and anchored in You. I give You my undivided attention, asking that distractions will not pull my heart away from seeking You fully.

I acknowledge that apart from You, I cannot walk in right standing. Fill me with Your Holy Spirit and make me aware of anything that keeps me from being truly hungry for You. Shape my desires so that they reflect Your will and draw me closer to Your heart.

In Jesus' name, Amen.

Song of Praise | Only You Can Satisfy / You Satisfy - Deeper Worship, William McDowell

Anchored at Night

A Safe Space

Anchoring Scripture

Psalm 91:1-2 (NIRV)

"Whoever rests in the shadow of the Most High God will be kept safe by the Mighty One. I will say about the Lord, 'He is my place of safety. He is like a fort to me. He is my God. I trust in him.'"

Anchoring Thought

There is a deep calm and peace in knowing that no matter what is happening in our world, we have assurance as followers and believers in Jesus Christ that we are never alone. God has promised that He will never leave us or forsake us.

To rest in God's shadow means that even in the darkest moments, His light covers and overshadows everything we face. When we dwell in the safety of the Most High, fear does not have the final word. We are held, protected, and cared for by a faithful God.

At the end of the day, we can release our worries, quiet our minds, and rest easily knowing we are safe in Him.

Night Prayer

Covered, calmed, and kept. Dear God, we come before You in Jesus' name, thanking You for the grace to surrender. Thank You for being our safe place and our covering. We trust that You will never leave us or forsake us.

Forgive us for the times we struggle to fully submit to Your will. Help us to yield every part of our hearts to You. Grant us wisdom and discernment to seek Your secret place and rest in Your peace.

Thank You that we are safe in Your arms. As we sleep, quiet our minds, restore our strength, and prepare us for what You will do. We trust You and praise You in advance. In Jesus' precious name, Amen.

Song of Praise | Safety (Part I) - LaCresia Campbell

Anchoring Reflections
Day 4

1. What worries or fears am I carrying into this night that God is inviting me to release into His care? Take a moment to name them honestly and imagine placing them under God's covering.

2. What does it look like for me to "dwell" in God's presence rather than just visit Him? How can I slow down, quiet my thoughts, and remain with God as I rest?

3. In what areas of my life am I still trying to protect myself instead of trusting God to be my refuge? What would surrender look like in this moment?

____

____

____

____

4. How does declaring "My God, in whom I trust" change the way I prepare my heart and mind for rest tonight? What promise from God can I hold onto as I fall asleep?

____

____

____

____

Day 5

HELP ME TO SEE ME

Anchored in the Morning

Anchoring Scripture

2 Peter 1:2–3 (NIV)

"Grace and peace be yours in abundance through the knowledge of God and of Jesus our Lord. His divine power has given us everything we need for a godly life through our knowledge of him who called us by his own glory and goodness."

Anchoring Thought

It is refreshing to know that, having been adopted through Christ, His compassion invites us into a godly way of living. Through that same compassion, God lovingly prunes us so that we can see what is truly within us—shaping our hearts and aligning our lives with His purpose. By His wonder-working power, our lives are transformed not through striving, but through knowing our Lord and Savior. As we grow in relationship with Him, we are also drawn into community with other believers who are growing in grace. Together, we become living witnesses of God's glory and goodness. It is by His power and grace that we begin to see ourselves as God sees us—called, equipped, and loved.

Anchoring Prayer
Strengthen and keep my heart, Lord. By Your divine power, help me to live godly and to see myself the way You see me. Holy Spirit, increase my capacity for You as I walk in the knowledge and grace to which I have been called. Shape my life to reflect Your will and Your purpose. In Jesus' name, Amen.

Song of Praise | I Am What You See - Pastor William H. Murphy III

Anchored at Night

I Shall Not Want

Anchoring Scripture

Psalm 33:20–22 (NIRV)

"We wait in hope for the Lord. He helps us. He is like a shield that keeps us safe. Our hearts are full of joy because of him. We trust in him, because he is holy. Lord, may your faithful love be with us. We put our hope in you."

Anchoring Thought

As this day comes to an end, I am reminded that my hope rests in the Lord. I am not lacking, because the One who helps me also shields me. When I place my trust in Him, my heart can rejoice—not because everything is perfect, but because God is faithful. Tonight, I release my worries and the need to control what comes next. I rest knowing that the Lord's unfailing love surrounds me as I trust in Him. In His care, I am provided for, protected, and held—so I can sleep in peace, confident that I shall not want.

Night Prayer

Dear Heavenly Father, I lay everything at Your feet tonight. I release my worries, my plans, and every distraction, and I choose to rest in You. Thank You for carrying me through this day and through this season. I trust that my heart and my will are safely surrendered to You. Lord, instruct my heart in the way of holiness, and let Your power guide me even in my weakness. I set my hope on You alone. I shall not want. I am not lacking, I am not alone, and I am not afraid. I rest knowing You are my help and my shield. In Jesus' name, Amen.

Song of Praise | Shall Not Want - Elevation Worship & Maverick City

Anchoring Reflections

Day 5

1.Where do I feel a sense of lack right now—and what would it look like to trust that God has already provided what I need?

How does believing "I shall not want" change how I view this area of my life?

2. How am I currently seeing myself: through fear and comparison, or through God's grace and truth?

What is God inviting me to notice about who I am becoming?

3. What am I still holding tightly that God is asking me to release tonight?

How does letting go help me rest more deeply and trust God more fully?

4. If I truly believed I am equipped, held, and loved by God, how would I move through tomorrow differently?

What step of faith or rest is God calling me to take next?

Day 6

PEACE LIKE A RIVER

Anchored in the Morning

Anchoring Scripture

Proverbs 3:1-2 (NIV)

"My son, do not forget my teaching, but keep my commands in your heart, for they will prolong your life many years and bring you peace and prosperity."

Anchoring Thought

The Hebrew word for wisdom is chokmah. It describes more than knowledge—it speaks to moral clarity and the ability to make right choices in everyday life. Wisdom, in this sense, is lived, practiced, and expressed through how we walk.

In the book of Proverbs, written primarily by King Solomon, we learn that true wisdom flows from obedience to God's Word. Solomon teaches that when God's instruction is followed and hidden in the heart, it produces peace, stability, and direction.

To follow God's Word is to walk in true wisdom. It is this wisdom we are invited to desire—not just for understanding, but so that our daily decisions reflect God's will and lead us into a life marked by peace and purpose.

Anchoring Prayer
Dear Lord, thank You for Your love and kindness and for the peace You give. Father, thank You for looking beyond my faults and providing for my needs. Even when my heart has not always been in tune with Your teaching and wisdom, I am grateful for Your grace that invites me into Your presence—where peace and wisdom abide.

Help me keep Your Word alive and active in my heart, so that I am free from oppressive thoughts, emotions, and worry. Teach me to cling to Your understanding and Your truth as You guide my life.
In Jesus' name, Amen.

Song of Praise | Always Peace - Brian Courtney Wilson

Anchored at Night

Anchored in Clarity

Anchoring Scripture

John 17:17-19 (NIRV)

"Use the truth to make them holy. Your word is truth. You sent me into the world. In the same way, I have sent them into the world. I make myself holy for them so that they too can be made holy by the truth."

Anchoring Thought

God's truth steadies me when my heart feels uncertain.

In turbulent times, it can be easy to accept what sounds like truth or to rely on what our hearts tell us. The challenge is that our hearts can be shaped by pain, deception, or self-interest, leading us toward our own version of truth instead of God's truth.

In John 17, we see Jesus in intimate conversation with the Father. In this prayer, Jesus intercedes on behalf of His people. His desire is clear—that they would be made holy and sanctified through the truth of God's Word.

Jesus reminds us that truth does not come from emotions or circumstances; it comes from God. As we rest, we are invited to release false narratives and allow God's Word to shape our hearts and minds. True clarity is found when we anchor ourselves in God's truth rather than our own understanding.

Night Prayer

Lord, You are great, and there is none like You. You are El Elyon, the Most High God. In a world searching for leadership, I thank You that I have You—my Lord, Savior, Redeemer, and King.

Give me clarity in this season. Do not let me ignore injustice or grow numb to what is happening around me. Help me reflect Jesus through integrity, kindness, and courage. Create sanctified spaces in my home, my workplace, and my church where Your love is felt and Your light is seen through me.

Keep my conviction steady so that I declare Your Word with truth and without compromise. Align my values with Your Spirit and guide me to move boldly where You are at work. Remind me that You are in control and that You never fail.

When heaviness surrounds me, I come to You for rest, trusting Your promise to carry what I cannot. Thank You for Your grace and mercy that hold me steady. In Jesus' name, Amen.

Song of Praise | Well, Well, Well - MAVHOUSE

Anchoring Reflections

Day 6

1. Where is God inviting me to rest in His peace instead of rushing for answers?

2. What truth from God's Word is bringing clarity to my thoughts right now?

3. What would it look like to let God's peace flow through me without resistance?

____

____

____

____

____

4. Am I trusting God's direction, or am I trying to control the current?

____

____

____

____

____

Day 7

ANCHORED FOR THE CALL

Anchored in the Morning

Anchoring Scripture

John 6:44 (NIV)

"No one can come to me unless the Father who sent me draws them, and I will raise them up at the last day."

Anchoring Thought

It is a privilege to be called by our Father. In this moment, Jesus addresses the people who were questioning His identity and grumbling about His words. He reminds them that any true attraction to Him—any divine call-ing—comes from God. Our desire to come to Christ is not self-generated; it is the work of God drawing us near.

Jesus makes this clear when He says, "And I, when I am lifted up from the earth, will draw all people to myself" (John 12:32).

It is in Him that we live, move, and have our being. Being called to Christ is the result of a transformed heart and mind, awakened by the Holy Spirit. The call is not based on our effort, understanding, or readiness—it is rooted in God's grace.

Our calling is not our own. We did not choose the call—God did. And our response is not striving, but obedience.

Anchoring Prayer

Heavenly Father, Prince of Peace, thank You for drawing us to Yourself. We recognize that our calling does not begin with us—it begins with You. Create in us pure hearts and renew within us a willing spirit to follow where You lead.

Anchor us in holiness, justice, mercy, and the truth of the Gospel. Help us walk in a way that honors You, remaining focused on the purpose You have placed before us. Strengthen us to stay faithful in prayer, grounded in Your Word, and connected in fellowship.

We trust that You have called us for this time and that You will empower us to reflect Your light wherever we go. We receive Your healing, transformation, and joy with faith and gratitude. In Jesus' name, Amen.

Song of Praise | The Call - Isabel Davis

Anchored at Night

Trusting Boldly

Anchoring Scripture

Hebrews 4:14-16 (NIRV)

"We have a great high priest. He has gone up into heaven. He is Jesus the Son of God. So let us hold firmly to what we say we believe. We have a high priest who can feel it when we are weak and hurting. We have a high priest who has been tempted in every way, just as we are. But he did not sin. So let us boldly approach God's throne of grace. Then we will receive mercy. We will find grace to help us when we need it."

Anchoring Thought

As Christians, we have a blessed assurance: even in seasons of pain and uncertainty, we are never without help. We have a High Priest—our Lord and Savior—who understands our weakness, sees us fully, and knows exactly what we need.

His grace is sufficient for us. It sustains us when we feel weary and strengthens us when we feel unsure. Because of Him, we are able to walk with boldness—not through our own strength, but by drawing near to God in prayer and placing our trust in Him.

Our confidence is not rooted in ourselves, but in Christ, who meets us with grace every time we come to Him.

Night Prayer

I find strength on my knees and confidence in Christ. Sovereign Lord, thank You for a fresh start and for Your grace that sustains me in every season. I surrender what has been holding me back and place my trust fully in You. You are the Author and Finisher of my faith, and You know what I need before I ask.

Help me trust You boldly, remain content where I am, and walk with wisdom and patience as I wait on Your timing. I believe You are faithful and that You are tearing down strongholds even now. I place everything in Your hands, withholding nothing. In Jesus' name, Amen.

Song of Praise | Trust In You - Anthony Brown & group therAPy

Anchoring Reflections

Day 7

1.Boldness

Where is God inviting me to walk in boldness right now?

2. Trust

How am I trusting Jesus, my High Priest, with my weakness and need today?

3. Obedience

What is God calling me to do in this season, and how can I respond in obedience?

4. Surrender

What am I still holding back, and what would it look like to surrender it fully to God?

Week 2: Anchored for a Fresh Anointing

STEADY WHILE GOD EQUIPS THIS SEASON

Day 8

TRUSTING GOD WITH MY TRANSFORMATION

Anchored in the Morning

Anchoring Scripture

Psalm 111:4-6 (NIRV)

"The Lord causes his wonders to be remembered. He is kind and tender. He provides food for those who have respect for him. He remembers his covenant forever. He has shown his people what his power can do. He has given them the lands of other nations."

Anchoring Thought

You may recognize this passage — we began Week 1 here. Return to it now with fresh eyes. What God showed you then and what He is showing you today are not the same. That is the nature of living Scripture.

This passage reminds us that the Lord's mighty works are beyond human understanding. His provision, His purposes, and His thoughts toward us are far greater than what our minds can fully comprehend. God's faithfulness invites us to trust Him even when we do not see the full picture.

We are reminded in John 3:16 that God so loved the world that He gave His only Son. If the God of the universe was willing to give everything for humanity, we can trust that He is more than capable of transforming our lives.

Trusting our transformation to the Most High God frees us from striving. As we walk in obedience and seek to live lives that please Him, we learn that this trust is not loss—it is great gain. When we lean on God and rest in His everlasting arms, He becomes our source, our strength, and our foundation.

Anchoring Prayer

I trust the God who gave everything to also transform everything. God Almighty, Lord of transformation and new beginnings, I come to You with gratitude. Thank You for showing up in my life and for working all things together, even in moments when I have been out of alignment.

As I prepare to walk into this new season, transform my heart and renew my mind. Forgive me for the times I have not fully leaned on You or trusted You with my transformation. I surrender the process to You and trust Your work in me. In Jesus' name, Amen.

Song of Praise | Impossible - Pastor Mike

Anchored at Night
Bold Worshiper

Anchoring Scripture

1 Chronicles 16:29 (NIRV)
"Praise the Lord for the glory that belongs to him. Bring an offering and come to him. Worship the Lord because of his beauty and holiness."

Anchoring Thought

In this Scripture of thanksgiving, King David offers praise to God simply for who He is. The offering he brings is not only material—it is surrender. David recognizes that the God we serve is worthy of all honor, reverence, and praise.

This passage reminds us that worship is an act of laying ourselves before the Lord. When we surrender our hearts, our worries, and our unfinished work to God, we are able to rest easily. Worship becomes the place where trust replaces striving and peace settles our souls.

Night Prayer

Father God, I come before You with gratitude for this day You have made. I adore You and stand in awe of who You are. Increase my boldness in worship, that I may worship You in spirit and in truth.

Let my life—my walk, my words, and my daily decisions—be an offering to You. Fix my heart so that my worship is not just spoken, but lived, honoring You fully and sincerely.

You are worthy of all praise. I surrender myself to You and thank You for shaping me into a true and bold worshiper. In Jesus' name, Amen.

Song of Praise | Worship Medley: I Worship You in the Spirit - Shek-inah Glory Ministry

Anchoring Reflections
Day 8

1.How am I trusting God with my transformation today?

2. What did boldness look like for me today—in my worship, my words, or my actions?

3. What change do I notice God beginning in me, even if it feels small?

4. You have made it through one full week. As you step into Week 2, what is something God showed you in Week 1 that you are carrying forward — and what is something you are choosing to leave behind?

Day 9

MY HOLY TEMPLE

Anchored in the Morning

Anchoring Scripture

1 Corinthians 3:16-17 (NIRV)

"Don't you know that you yourselves are God's temple? Don't you know that God's Spirit lives among you? If anyone destroys God's temple, God will destroy that person. God's temple is holy. And you all together are that temple."

Anchoring Thought

In this passage, Paul reminds the believers in Corinth that they are God's temple and that God's Spirit lives within them. This truth is not symbolic—it is sacred. God has chosen to dwell among His people, making their lives holy and set apart for Him.

Paul emphasizes how deeply God values His dwelling place. Because the Spirit of God lives within us, our lives are honored and protected by God Himself. What belongs to God is not disposable or overlooked—it is cherished.

You can rest knowing that your body is God's holy temple. You are sacred, held in His care, and ready to be used for His purposes.

Anchoring Prayer

Our Father in heaven, we give You all honor and praise for who You are and for all You have done. We repent for the ways we have not honored our temples or aligned our hearts with Your Word.

Holy Spirit, search us and shape us. Make us into a sanctuary—pure, holy, and set apart for Your glory. We surrender to Your hands as the Potter, trusting the work You are doing within us.

Unite us as Your people, called for such a time as this, to build Your holy temple in obedience and love. We bow before You with humbled hearts, giving You all the glory. In Jesus' name, Amen.

Song of Praise | My Tribute (To God Be The Glory) - Natalie Grant feat. CeCe Winans

Anchored at Night
Anchored in Mercy

Anchoring Scripture

Lamentations 3:22-23 (NKJV)

"Through the Lord's mercies we are not consumed, Because His compassions fail not. They are new every morning; Great is Your faithfulness."

Anchoring Thought

Throughout history—and even today—there have always been wars, rumors of wars, and seasons of hardship. Life often feels like a cycle of storms: storms of grief, financial burdens, family tension, marriage struggles, or work-related pressures. These experiences can feel overwhelming and heavy, weighing down our hearts.

Yet the book of Lamentations reminds us of a powerful truth spoken in the midst of deep sorrow: because of the Lord's great love, we are not consumed. God's compassion does not fail, and His mercies are renewed every single morning. Even in times of loss, confusion, and pain, God remains faithful.

This promise becomes our anchor. When everything around us feels uncertain, God's mercy holds us steady. Each new day brings fresh grace, allowing our hearts to rest—not because the storm has ended, but because God's faithfulness has not.

Night Prayer

God's mercy is new today, and it is enough for me. O Lord, how excellent is Your name in all the earth. You are the God who commands Your angels to keep watch over me day and night. I thank You for my daily bread and for manna from above.

I thank You that Your love pursues me and that Your goodness and mercy follow me all the days of my life. I repent of my transgressions and rest in Your mercy, which delivers me from iniquity and holds me steady when life feels uncertain.

Anchor my heart in Your love so that I am not moved by fear or doubt. Help me rest in Your presence, trust in Your promises, and extend grace and mercy to others.

Keep me grounded in prayer, in Your Word, in peace, and in compassion. I place this night in Your care. In Jesus' name, Amen.

Song of Praise | Chasing Me Down - Israel & New Breed ft. Tye Tribbett

Anchoring Reflections
Day 9

1.How have I experienced God's mercy toward my body, heart, or mind today?

2. In what ways has God shown me grace where I felt weak, tired, or unworthy?

3. How am I honoring God's presence within me as His holy temple?

4. What part of my life is God inviting me to care for with more gentleness and mercy?

Day 10

PROCLAIMING BOLDLY

Anchored in the Morning

Anchoring Scripture

Ephesians 6:19–20 (NIRV)

"Pray also for me. Pray that whenever I speak, the right words will be given to me. Then I can be bold as I tell the mystery of the good news. Because of the good news, I am being held by chains as the Lord's messenger. So pray that I will be bold as I preach the good news. That's what I should do."

Anchoring Thought

Paul asks the church to pray for him because he understands that true boldness does not come from human strength, position, or confidence—it comes from the Spirit of God. Even while in chains, Paul desires clarity and courage to proclaim the good news of Christ faithfully.

He reminds us that following Christ comes with a cost. Discipleship may include suffering, discomfort, and sacrifice, yet the good news is this: we do not walk this path alone. We have a High Priest who understands suffering and whose power works through us, even in difficult circumstances.

Through the Spirit of God, boldness is formed—not to draw attention to ourselves, but to faithfully proclaim Christ. No matter the chains, no matter the season, God's power empowers us to go and share the gospel with courage and truth.

Anchoring Prayer

Heavenly Father, I thank You for Your mercy, grace, and faithfulness toward me. I recognize that boldness does not come from me, but from Your Spirit at work within me.

Give me the words to speak and the courage to proclaim the gospel clearly and without fear. Strengthen me to live in a way that reflects Christ, so that my life points others to You.

I count it a privilege to be called by You, and I choose to walk in obedience—trusting You to work through me for Your glory. In Jesus' name, Amen.

Song of Praise | Be Still and Know - CeCe Winans

Anchored at Night
Anchored in Forgiveness

Anchoring Scripture

Colossians 3:13 (NIV)

"Bear with each other and forgive one another if any of you has a grievance against someone. Forgive as the Lord forgave you."

Anchoring Thought

The fullness of God invites us to rest and to release anything in our hearts that would hinder us from sharing the good news—especially unforgiveness. God is a forgiving God, and through His grace, He empowers us to forgive others just as He has forgiven us.

Scripture reminds us that forgiveness brings freedom. It keeps our hearts from becoming bitter and our spirits from being weighed down. When we release offense, we make room for God's fullness to dwell within us, allowing our lives to reflect His love with clarity and grace. Forgiveness is not weakness—it is a gift that frees us to live and love as God intended.

Night Prayer

Forgiveness clears my heart so God's fullness can flow through me. Heavenly Father, my Light and my Salvation, I thank You for Your grace and mercy that carry me each day. You go before me and make my path straight, and I give You all the glory.

You forgive me when I fall short—help me to forgive others as You have forgiven me. Search my heart and remove any unforgiveness. Teach me to walk in the freedom that comes from surrender and grace.

Help me choose love over offense, peace over bitterness, and unity over division. Anchor my heart in forgiveness so that I may walk in peace and reflect Your love. In Jesus' name, Amen.

Song of Praise | Broken But I'm Healed - Byron Cage

Anchoring Reflections
Day 10

1. What am I laying at God's feet tonight?

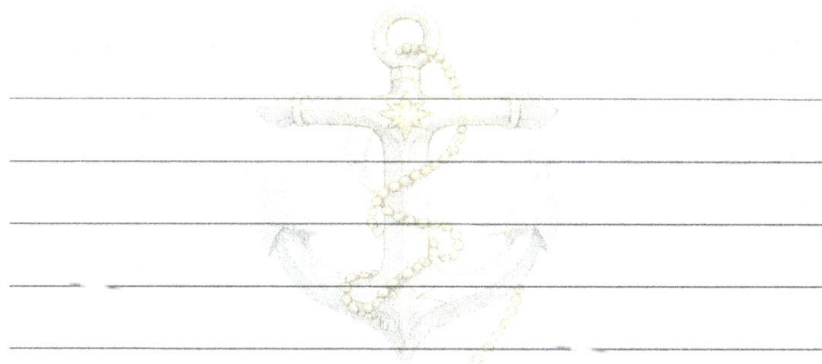

2. Where am I trusting God to help me walk in boldness?

3. What am I releasing into God's care tonight?

4. What do I need to forgive, or release, so that I can walk in greater freedom?

5. Day 10 is about proclaiming boldly — not just believing quietly. Where in your life right now is God inviting you to move from private faith to public declaration? What has been holding you back, and what would one bold step look like today?

Day 11

It's Bigger Than Me

Anchored in the Morning

Anchoring Scripture

Isaiah 40:31 (NIV)

"But those who hope in the Lord will renew their strength. They will soar on wings like eagles; they will run and not grow weary, they will walk and not be faint."

Anchoring Thought

Waiting on the Lord is not always easy, especially when the weight of life feels heavy and weariness sets in. There are moments when it feels as though the anchor is slipping and strength is fading. Yet Isaiah reminds us to remain steady and trust God in the waiting.

Those who hope in the Lord are not abandoned or forgotten. God renews strength when we choose to wait, not rush. The same God who began a good work in you is faithful to sustain you through it. As we wait on Him, we are given strength to rise, to walk, and to run with endurance.

Anchoring Prayer

Father, I thank You for always being near, covering me, and caring for me. Help me to wait well, to be patient, faithful, and not grow weary in doing good.

Teach me to trust You instead of worrying or complaining. In my waiting, help me to praise You in all things, knowing that You see the full picture and are guiding me on the best path for my life.

As I wait, help me to listen for Your voice, to serve others with love, to give generously, and to pray continually. Thank You for hearing my prayers and for being mindful of me. I love You, Lord, and I depend on You fully. In Jesus' name, Amen.

Song of Praise | Wait On You - Elevation Worship & Maverick City

Anchored at Night
Anchored to Sow

Anchoring Scripture

2 Corinthians 9:6 (NIRV)

"Here is something to remember. The one who plants only a little will gather only a little. And the one who plants a lot will gather a lot."

Anchoring Thought

The apostle Paul reminds the church in Corinth that sowing is not only about how much we give, but what we give. Sowing without purpose yields little fruit, but sowing what carries eternal value produces obedience, growth, and lasting legacy.

This kind of sowing requires grace and discernment. We seek the Lord for wisdom to know when, where, and how to sow, anchoring our lives in what will yield eternal fruit. God is not calling us to sow recklessly, but faithfully—focused not on quantity alone, but on quality that reflects His purpose. What is planted in obedience, God multiplies with intention.

Night Prayer

I choose to sow with purpose and trust God with the harvest. Dear Heavenly Father, God of the harvest, I thank You for Your faithfulness, Your promises, and for anchoring me in Your love.

Forgive me for the times I have not sown generously with my life. Teach me to plant seeds of the Spirit—love, peace, patience, and faith—so that my life may bear fruit that blesses others.

Guard my heart from fear and weariness. Anchor my hope in You, firm and secure, as I rest tonight. Thank You for entrusting me with gifts to be used for

Your Kingdom and for the harvest You will bring through obedience. I place this night in Your hands. In Jesus' name, Amen.

Song of Praise | Faithful Is Our God - Hezekiah Walker

Anchoring Reflections

Day 11

1.What is God asking me to release because this season is bigger than my strength, control, or understanding?

2. What am I sowing in my life right now—with my time, words, or actions?

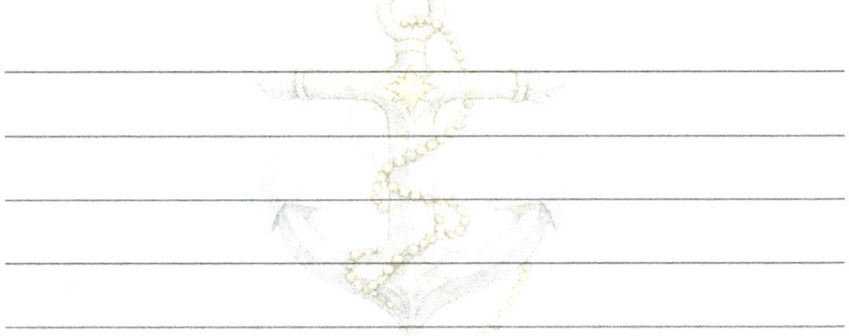

3. Is what I am sowing aligned with God's purpose and eternal value?

4. What fear, weariness, or hesitation do I need to release so I can sow in faith?

5. Where do I trust God to bring the harvest, even if I don't see it yet?

Day 12

ANCHORED IN KINGDOM

Anchored in the Morning

Anchoring Scripture

Acts 19:8 (NIRV)

"Paul entered the synagogue. There he spoke boldly for three months. He gave good reasons for believing the truth about God's kingdom."

Anchoring Thought

Paul, called by Christ and once a persecutor of believers, becomes obedient to the charge given to him—the same charge given to all of us: to go and make disciples. Despite persecution and hardship, Paul is confident in his calling and faithful to his purpose.

In the book of Acts, Paul is deeply committed to building the Church—the body of Christ made up of many gifts, working together for God's glory. He takes Kingdom work seriously, boldly speaking the truth of the gospel and preparing hearts to receive the good news of God's Kingdom.

Paul's life reminds us that the Kingdom of God lives within us and is meant to be expressed through how we live and act here on earth. To be anchored in the Kingdom is to walk in obedience, purpose, and faithfulness to God's call.

Anchoring Prayer

Father God, I thank You for calling me and for the gift of the Holy Spirit. I ask for a fresh anointing over my life so that I may walk boldly in the gifts You have placed within me, for the building of Your Kingdom.

I decree that I am obedient to Your call and faithful to the charge to make disciples. I speak life over myself, my family, my church, and my community. I decree that I walk with purpose, clarity, and courage as I proclaim the truth of the gospel.

I decree that I am not moved by opposition or fear, but strengthened by Your grace. I declare that I will run my race with endurance, remain committed to holiness and righteousness, and stand firm in declaring Your Word with love and truth.

I decree that Your Kingdom lives within me and is revealed through my actions here on earth. I trust You for the victory, the fruit, and the fulfillment of what You have begun. In Jesus' name, Amen.

Song of Praise | Kingdom - Maverick City Music (feat. Naomi Raine & Chandler Moore)

Anchored at Night
Anchored in Devotion

Anchoring Scripture

Matthew 22:37 (NIV)
"Jesus replied: 'Love the Lord your God with all your heart and with all your soul and with all your mind.'"

Anchoring Thought

The Gospel of Matthew gives close attention to the Kingdom of God as a matter of the heart. Kingdom living begins with a surrendered heart posture—one that relies on God to shape our hearts, minds, and souls according to His will.

We love the Lord because God first loved us. As we surrender to His way, our devotion is formed and strengthened. This surrender creates a heart posture that keeps us anchored—devoted in prayer, faithful in service, and rooted in love for our Lord and Savior, Jesus Christ.

As children of the King, our devotion is lived out daily. It is an unspoken vow expressed through obedience, worship, and wholehearted love for God.

Night Prayer

Gracious Father, I thank You for Your steadfast love, faithfulness, and new mercies. You keep Your promises, and I trust Your Word.

Purify my heart and mind, Lord, and deepen my devotion to You. I choose to love You with all my heart, soul, and mind. Anchor my life in You and order my steps so I may walk in Your will.

Help me remain devoted to seeking You, serving You, and living for Your glory. Keep my heart from growing weary, and strengthen me to stay faithful to the call You have placed on my life.

I give You all the honor and praise. In Jesus' name, Amen.

Song of Praise | Satisfied Reprise - Jordan G. Welch

Anchoring Reflections

Day 12

1.How is God inviting me to live for His Kingdom in my everyday actions?

2. What does loving God with all my heart, soul, and mind look like in this season?

3. Where do I need to surrender more fully so my devotion can grow deeper?

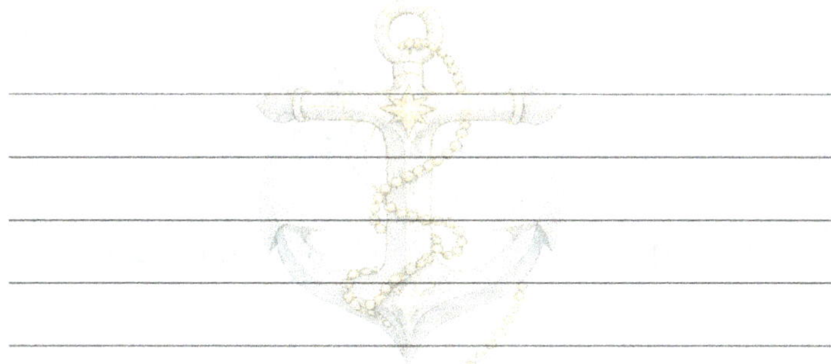

4. How can my prayer life, service, and love better reflect my devotion to Christ?

Day 13

ANOINTED FOR THE JOURNEY

Anchored in the Morning

Anchoring Scripture

Ephesians 2:10 (NIV)

"For we are God's handiwork, created in Christ Jesus to do good works, which God prepared in advance for us to do."

Anchoring Thought

Paul reminds the church in Ephesus of their new identity in Christ. Once dead, they now have life. As new creations, they are not wandering without purpose, but are God's workmanship—created intentionally and formed with care.

Paul teaches that we were created to do good works that God prepared in advance. We are equipped for the journey set before us, not by chance, but by divine design. This truth invites us to walk confidently, trusting that God has already gone ahead of us.

Let us hold fast to our calling, remembering that we were created with purpose and anointed for the journey God has prepared.

Anchoring Prayer
Our Father and Savior, Lord of all, thank You for Your power and Your grace that sustains us. We praise You for creating us with purpose and for giving us strength to stand firm and not be shaken.

As we walk this journey, help us not to grow weary in doing good. Fill us with Your Spirit, granting us peace, courage, and discernment to follow where You lead. Remind us that every step we take is guided by You.

Help us to be attentive to Your voice through prayer and Your Word, and obedient to the calling You have placed on our lives. Prepare us to share the gospel with those You place in our path.

We trust You to lead us forward. In Jesus' name, Amen.

Song of Praise | You Are My Champion - Dante Bowe / Bethel Music

Anchored at Night
Anchored in Intention

Anchoring Scripture

Psalm 16:8 (NIRV)

"I keep my eyes always on the Lord. He is at my right hand. So I will always be secure."

Anchoring Thought

This psalm of trust reminds us that God is intentional about keeping His children secure. When we keep the Lord before us, we are not easily shaken, because He stands at our right hand—our source of strength, authority, and protection.

Scripture teaches that God equips us to stand firm against what comes against us, covering us with His truth and strength day and night. Because God is intentional about us, we are called to be intentional in our devotion to Him—fixing our eyes on the Lord and aligning our lives with His will.

When we keep our focus on God, we walk with confidence, knowing that the Highest Authority goes before us and holds us steady through every season of the journey.

Night Prayer

I keep the Lord always before me, and I am not shaken. Our Father in Heaven, we stand in awe of You. Your power, glory, and love guide us each day. By Your Spirit, You breathe life into us and keep us anchored in hope.

Lord, because You are intentional with us, help us to live intentionally before You—walking in Your light so that others may see You through our lives.

Strengthen our faith and steady our hearts with the peace that surpasses all understanding, no matter what surrounds us.

As we move through this week, help us remain intentional in prayer, in Your Word, and in worship. Keep our eyes fixed on You, trusting that You will give us strength, focus, and direction.

We choose to walk with purpose and give You all the glory, believing You for continued victory. In Jesus' name, Amen.

Song of Praise | Intentional - Travis Greene

Anchoring Reflections

Day 13

1.Where is God inviting me to move with greater intention instead of habit?

2. How is God's anointing showing up in my journey right now, even in small ways?

Anchoring Reflections

Day 13

3. What do I need to lay down so I can walk fully in the purpose God has prepared for me?

4. How can I keep my eyes fixed on God as I continue this journey, trusting Him to lead each step?

Day 14

Anchored in Commitment

Anchored in the Morning

Anchoring Scripture

Proverbs 16:3 (NIV)

"Commit to the Lord whatever you do, and he will establish your plans."

Anchoring Thought

The book of Proverbs is known for guiding us toward wise living and away from paths that lead to destruction. In this passage, Solomon invites us to trust and honor God with all our plans by committing them fully to Him.

When we move forward without God, we risk self-reliance—depending on our own strength and understanding instead of God's wisdom and eternal perspective. True commitment begins with surrender. As we submit our plans to the Lord, He establishes them, not just for success, but for lasting purpose and legacy.

Committing our ways to God keeps us anchored in the process, trusting that He knows the full weight and value of what He has called us to do.

Anchoring Prayer

Dear Lord, thank You for placing me on the path You have prepared for my life. Thank You for Your wisdom, authority, and power that see the eternal value in every plan.

Forgive me for the times I rely on my own strength instead of trusting You. Lead and guide my plans so they bless not only me, but also those connected to my life and legacy.

I commit my ways to You. Let every strategy be ordained by You. In Jesus' name, Amen.

Song of Praise | My Life Is In Your Hands - Maverick City Music x Kirk Franklin

Anchored at Night

Near the Cross

Anchoring Scripture

Luke 9:23 (NIRV)

"Then he said to all of them, 'Whoever wants to follow me must say no to themselves. They must pick up their cross every day and follow me.'"

Anchoring Thought

The cross is the ultimate sign of steadfast love, sacrifice, and the promise given to all who follow Christ. It is both a place of surrender—where we lay down our burdens—and a reminder that following Jesus includes sacrifice.

At the cross, Jesus declared, "If I am lifted up, I will draw all people to myself" (John 12:32, NIV). Our identity as followers of Christ is inseparable from the cross. To carry our cross is to accept the call of discipleship, understanding that we cannot walk this journey in our old ways or former selves.

Carrying the cross means putting on the new life—the disciple who follows Christ in obedience and humility. It is not a burden of shame, but an honor of devotion. To be near the cross is to choose daily surrender, allowing Christ to shape who we are and how we live.

Night Prayer

Lord Jesus, I thank You for calling me into discipleship. As I draw near to the cross, help me to deny myself, take up my cross daily, and follow You with an obedient heart.

Teach me to lay down my own ways and surrender my plans to You. Give me strength to follow You even when it costs my comfort, convenience, or control.

Form me into a faithful disciple who loves well, serves humbly, and walks in obedience to Your Word. Strengthen me where I am weak, and help me commit all my ways to You.

I choose to follow You—daily and fully. In Jesus' name, Amen.

Song of Praise | At The Cross - CeCe Winans

Anchoring Reflections
Day 14

1.What is God inviting me to lay down as an act of commitment to Him?

2. In what area of my life do I need to deny myself and fully trust Christ?

3. How am I taking up my cross daily in my thoughts, choices, or actions?

4. What does following Jesus with obedience and love look like for me right now?

Week 3:
Anchored and Awakened

FAITH-ROOTED AND SPIRITUALLY ALERT

Day 15

ANCHORING PAUSE

Anchored in the Morning

Anchoring Scripture

John 1:1 (KJV)

"In the beginning was the Word, and the Word was with God, and the Word was God."

Anchoring Thought

Pause & Reflect — Preparing for Week 3.

Before I try to understand everything God is doing, I rest in who God is.

As Week 3 approaches, this is a sacred time to pause and reflect on what God has been stirring within you. Today is an invitation to rest in the breath of God through His Word—to slow down, to listen, and to simply be in His presence.

Take time to revisit your reflections, sit with the Scriptures, and even worship through song. Allow yourself to rest in what God, through His amazing grace, has revealed and carried you through so far. Anchored in the Weeds was not designed to be rushed through, but to be walked with. It is meant to be a companion—an invitation to go deeper, to linger with God, and to allow Him to examine your heart.

This is a time for holy reflection. A time to ask God to search you, to reveal what needs healing, surrender, or renewal. Let this pause be gentle. Let it be honest. Let it be sacred.

Before I try to understand everything God is doing, I rest in who God is.

Special Invitation:

If you are reading this and have not yet accepted God as your Lord and Savior, know that this moment can be the beginning. You can repent, ask God for forgiveness, and place your trust in Him. The Word of God promises that if you believe in your heart and confess with your mouth, you will be saved.

Let today be a pause. Let it be reflection. Let it be lament, if needed. And let it be a resting place in God's presence.

Anchoring Prayer

Lord, in Your infinite wisdom and mighty power, You have allowed me to draw near to You, and for that I am grateful. During this pause, anchor my heart and mind in the remembrance of Your Word and in who You are.

Give me the strength to hold fast to Your hope and the grace to finish strong. As I continue this journey, keep me open and attentive to Your divine Word and Your leading.

I rest in You and trust You with what lies ahead. In Jesus' name, Amen.

Song of Praise | Psalm 23 (I Am Not Alone) - People & Songs

Anchored at Night
Resting in the Pause

Anchoring Scripture

Psalm 46:10 (NIV)

"He says, 'Be still, and know that I am God; I will be exalted among the nations, I will be exalted in the earth.'"

Anchoring Thought

As this day of reflection comes to a close, we are reminded of the simple yet profound command to "be still." The journey of faith is not only about moving forward; it is also about learning to rest in the presence of the One who holds it all together.

Tonight, release the need to strive, to plan, or to fully understand what comes next. Allow the truths God has revealed to you over these past two weeks to settle deeply into your spirit. You are held, you are loved, and you can rest securely in the knowledge that He is God.

Night Prayer

Heavenly Father, thank You for the gift of this pause and for the gentle reminder to simply be in Your presence. As I quiet my heart tonight, help me to rest in Your peace and trust in Your perfect timing. Silence the noise of my own understanding and anchor my soul in Your grace. I surrender my questions, my weariness, and my plans to You. Keep me securely in Your hands as I sleep, preparing me for the week ahead. In Jesus' name, Amen.

Song of Praise | Be Still - Hillsong Worship

Anchoring Reflections

Day 15

Take your time. Sit with each question without rushing.

1.Revelation

What has God revealed to me about Himself during these first fourteen days?

2. Understanding

How has my understanding of being anchored—in faith, obedience, and devotion—changed?

3. Commitment

What has God asked me to surrender or commit more fully to Him?

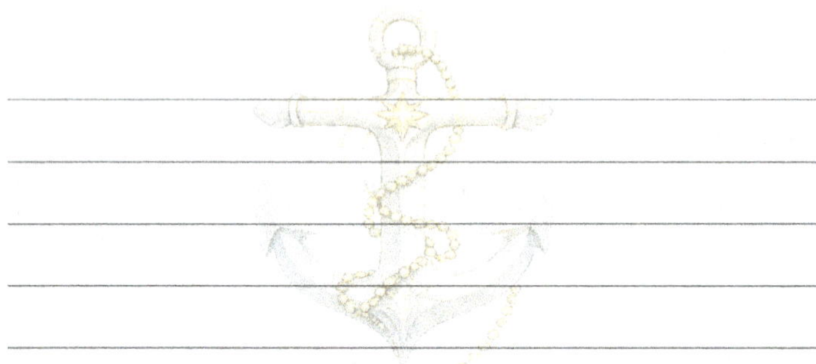

4. Growth

Where have I noticed growth, clarity, or renewed strength in my spiritual walk?

5. Invitation

What do I sense God inviting me into as I continue this journey forward?

Day 16

ANCHORED IN SIGHT

Anchored in the Morning

Anchoring Scripture

Matthew 13:13 (NIRV)

"Here is why I use stories when I speak to the people. I say, 'They look, but they don't really see. They listen, but they don't really hear or understand.'"

Anchoring Thought

The Bible speaks of sight both physically and spiritually. Physical sight is seen in Scripture from the very beginning—in Genesis through the creation story—and throughout the Gospels when Jesus heals the blind and restores vision. Scripture also speaks of sight metaphorically, through faith, prophetic vision, spiritual awakening, and insight.

In the Gospel of Matthew, Jesus reminds us that it is possible to see and yet not truly perceive, to hear and yet not understand. True sight is a gift from the Lord. This mercy is given to the people of God not so we can be the smartest in the room, but so we can keep our eyes on His way, His timing, His wisdom, and His truth.

When we remain anchored in spiritual sight—humble, attentive, and surrendered—we are kept from confusion and falling. Keeping our eyes on the Lord allows us to walk in obedience with clarity, even when everything is not fully seen.

Anchoring Prayer

Lord, give me eyes that truly see and a heart that understands. Dear God, Lord of sight—Jehovah El Roi, the God who sees me—I thank You for the gift of insight and foresight. As I walk this journey, help me use the vision You give for the upbuilding of Your Kingdom.

Keep my eyes fixed on You. Let my life reflect the goodness of the One who graciously sees me and knows my way. Grant me clear sight, humble discernment, and a heart that remains aligned with Your truth.

Thank You in advance for Your forgiving power and for the wisdom You provide each step of the way. In Jesus' name, Amen.

Song of Praise | As The Deer - Jordan G. Welch

Anchored at Night
Joy in My Soul

Anchoring Scripture

1 Peter 1:5–6 (NIRV)
"Through faith you are kept safe by God's power. Your salvation is going to be completed. It is ready to be shown to you in the last days. Because you know all this, you have great joy."

Anchoring Thought
Joy is a product of faith. It is the assurance that my inner being does not need circumstances to align in order to experience joy. True joy is not dependent on what is happening around me—it is rooted in what I believe.

This blessed assurance reminds me that even in heartache, suffering, and moments of happiness, my true center remains Jesus. My joy comes from the promise that I am not forsaken. It is anchored in the safety and hope found in Christ—who gave His life for my sins and continues to intercede for me, sanctifying and sustaining my soul.

This truth steadies my heart. It is what anchors me in joy that cannot be shaken.

Night Prayer
Father, Lord of hope and mercy, I thank You for loving me and choosing grace over judgment. Because of You, my joy is not rooted in circumstances, but in faith.

Even when I do not see everything clearly, I trust You. As Your Word says, I rejoice with a joy that is inexpressible and full of glory, knowing that my faith in You anchors my soul and secures my salvation.

Guard my heart from comparison and heaviness. Clothe me with praise, help me slow down, and allow me to find joy in You—even in the ordinary moments of this day.

My joy is in You alone. In Jesus' name, Amen.

Song of Praise | Joy of the Lord - Maverick City Music (feat. Katie Torwalt, Dante Bowe & Mav City Gospel Choir)

Anchoring Reflections

Day 16

1.Where might God be inviting me to see with spiritual eyes rather than rely only on what is visible?

2. What has God revealed to me recently that has strengthened my faith or brought clarity?

3. How does fixing my heart on Christ shape the joy I carry, even when circumstances are uncertain?

____

____

____

____

4. Where can I choose faith today so my joy remains anchored rather than shaken?

____

____

____

____

Day 17

ANCHORED IN LIBERATION

Anchored in the Morning
Anchoring Scripture

Galatians 5:1 (NIV)
"It is for freedom that Christ has set us free. Stand firm, then, and do not let yourselves be burdened again by a yoke of slavery."

Anchoring Thought
Freedom, as Scripture teaches it, is not a vacation from responsibility or obligation as the world defines it. The freedom Paul speaks of to the church

in Galatia is far deeper. It is the freedom found in Christ—the freedom that brings forgiveness of sins, new life, and true liberation.

This freedom delivers us from bondage and releases us from the darkness that comes from living apart from Christ. In Jesus, we are no longer enslaved by sin, shame, or fear. We are freed to live in the light, to walk in obedience, and to stand firm in the grace that has been given to us.

Anchored in this freedom, we are no longer bound—we are restored, renewed, and invited into a life of lasting hope.

Anchoring Prayer

Dear Lord, I worship and adore You. You are my freedom, my source, and my peace. Because of You, I am no longer bound, but free to live in the abundance of Your love.

Thank You for saving me and anchoring me in truth. I was once lost, but You rescued me and gave me a new life. Help me never forget where You brought me from.

Give me wisdom to walk in freedom and to share Your love with those still seeking it. Teach me to walk daily in the gospel of peace, so that wherever I go, Your presence is felt.

I stand firm in the freedom You have given me. In Jesus' name, Amen.

Song of Praise | Freedom Song - Maranda Curtis

Anchored at Night
Joy in God's Love

Anchoring Scripture

Zephaniah 3:17 (NIRV)

"The Lord your God is with you. He is the Mighty Warrior who saves. He will take great delight in you. In his love he will no longer punish you. Instead, he will sing for joy because of you."

Anchoring Thought

During the time of Zephaniah, injustice and unrest were widespread, and the people were called into a season of renewal. Zephaniah's message reminded them that God was not distant—He was with them, thinking about them, and actively moving on their behalf.

This is the delight Zephaniah speaks of: God's love is not rooted in punishment, but in loving conviction. His correction flows from care, restoration, and a deep desire for His people to return to Him. God's love reassures us that even in difficult seasons, we are seen, held, and remembered.

Our God desires us to be rooted in joy—not only for our strength, but because our joy brings Him pleasure. As we worship Him in trust and confidence, He delights in us so deeply that He rejoices over us with singing. This is the joy of belonging to a God who loves His people with joy.

Night Prayer

Father, my Wonderful Counselor, my Shepherd, and my Refuge, I praise You with my whole heart. Thank You for being with me, for surrounding me with Your love, and for quieting my fears by Your presence.

I stand in awe knowing that You rejoice over me with gladness and sing over my life with joy. Your love sustains me through every season, and Your strength carries me from glory to glory.

Help me delight in You, rest in Your love, and walk confidently in who You have called me to be. You are my everlasting portion, and I trust You completely. In Jesus' name, Amen.

Song of Praise | How He Loves - Anthony Evans

Anchoring Reflections

Day 17

1.Where have I experienced freedom in Christ, and how am I choosing to stand firm in that freedom?

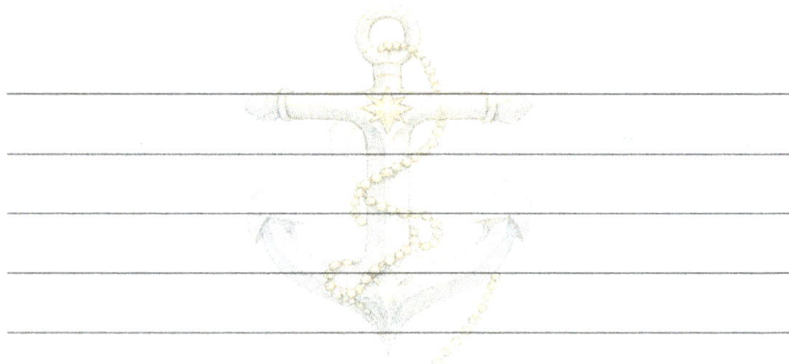

2. What is God inviting me to release so I can walk more fully in the liberty He has given me?

3. How does knowing that God delights in me and rejoices over me with love affect how I see myself?

____

____

____

____

____

4. In what ways can I allow God's joy over my life to quiet fear, shame, or heaviness today?

____

____

____

____

____

Day 18

ANCHORED IN COMMUNITY

Anchored in the Morning

Anchoring Scripture

Ecclesiastes 4:9-10 (NIRV)

"Two people are better than one. They can help each other in everything they do. Suppose either of them falls down. Then the one can help the other one up. But suppose a person falls down and doesn't have anyone to help them up. Then feel sorry for that person!"

Anchoring Thought

This book of wisdom teaches us that life was never meant to be lived alone, and that the success of life is deeply connected to who God allows us to walk with. From the very beginning, God revealed this design by blessing Adam with Eve. Community was not an afterthought—it was part of creation.

Throughout the Bible, we see how God blesses people through relationships. Even Jesus, who has all power and authority, chose to walk alongside twelve disciples. He did not need them, yet He invited them in to show that the work of the Kingdom is done together, not in isolation.

God blesses us individually so that we can be strengthened collectively. David had Nathan to guide and correct him, and Barak had Deborah to help him lead with courage and wisdom.

We need one another—not just to succeed, but to survive and fulfill the work God has placed before us.

Anchoring Prayer

Heavenly Father, my Lord and Savior, I thank You for the gift of community and for reminding me that I am not meant to walk this journey alone. Your Word teaches me that as iron sharpens iron, I am strengthened through godly relationships.

Help me to be someone who encourages, sharpens, and builds others up in love. Teach me to live as a true disciple—following You faithfully and reflecting Christ through my words and actions.

Where there has been division, bring unity. Where there has been hurt, bring healing. Anchor me in Your truth and keep me accountable so that love may grow, faith may deepen, and hope may abound.

In Jesus' name, Amen.

Song of Praise | Make Us One - ft. Naomi Raine

Anchored at Night

Love for My Neighbor

Anchoring Scripture
1 John 4:21 (NIRV)
"Here is the command God has given us. Anyone who loves God must also love their brother and sister."

Anchoring Thought

In 1 John, the writer addresses a community struggling to fully acknowledge who Jesus Christ is—both Savior and divine authority. Alongside this, they needed a clear reminder: loving Jesus cannot be separated from loving others. This command is not optional.

Scripture makes it plain that those who claim to love Christ must also love people. Love is not passive or silent. It speaks up against injustice, defends the vulnerable, and stands with the marginalized. When believers fail to speak out against the mistreatment of children, immigrants, and oppressed communities, they fall short of the call of discipleship.

This text reminds us that love is the visible mark of a true follower of Christ. Without love in action, our confession of faith is incomplete. To follow Jesus is to love boldly, justly, and without condition.

Night Prayer

Dear Lord, thank You for Your grace and mercy that follow me daily. I repent for the times I have failed to love my neighbor fully or to speak up on their behalf. Fill me with Your Holy Spirit so that my thoughts, actions, and love align with who You are. Teach me to steward my relationships well and to love others as You have commanded.

Help my love to be active, faithful, and true.
In Jesus' name, Amen.

Song of Praise | Jesus Is Love - Heather Headley

Anchoring Reflections

Day 18

1.Who has God placed in my life to walk alongside me, and how am I showing up as a support to them?

2. In what ways am I actively loving my neighbor, not just with words, but through my actions?

3. Where have I been silent when love required me to speak up, stand up, or intervene?

____

____

____

____

____

4. How can I steward my relationships with greater compassion, accountability, and Christ-like love?

____

____

____

____

Day 19

ANCHORED IN PEACE

Anchored in the Morning

Anchoring Scripture

Isaiah 26:3 (NIRV)

"Lord, you will give perfect peace
to those who commit themselves to be faithful to you.
That's because they trust in you."

Anchoring Thought
Isaiah offers a word of victory to Israel, reminding them that even in times of

war, famine, and unsettling circumstances, there is a peace the world cannot give or take away. This peace surpasses human understanding and is found in trusting the Lord completely. Those who commit themselves fully to God and His plan are kept in perfect peace—not because life is easy, but because their minds are stayed on Him. Let us remain determined and unwavering in our faith, choosing to trust the Lord as our everlasting Rock.

Anchoring Prayer

Father, thank You for knowing me fully and for caring for every part of my life. I receive the peace You give—peace that surpasses understanding and steadies me even when outcomes are uncertain. Help me keep my mind stayed on You and trust You as my everlasting Rock. Align my heart and spirit with Yours, and guard my thoughts so I may walk in freedom and wholeness. I praise You for Your covering and strength each day. Keep me in Your peace, and I will remain secure. In Jesus' name, Amen.

Song of Praise | Perfect Peace - Marvin Sapp

Anchored at Night
Anchored in Formation

Anchoring Scripture

2 Corinthians 3:18 (NIRV)

"None of our faces are covered with a veil. All of us can see the Lord's glory and think deeply about it. So we are being changed to become more like Him so that we have more and more glory. And this glory comes from the Lord, who is the Holy Spirit."

Anchoring Thought

The glory of God is His holy power that rests, rules, and abides within us. This glory does not come and go—it is at work in us, continually forming and sanctifying us as we become more like Christ. From glory to glory, the Holy Spirit is shaping our hearts, our character, and our faith. Let us not grow weary when we are tested or when it feels as though God's glory has shifted. Instead, let us hold fast to the truth that the Holy Spirit is present and at work for us, forming us even in seasons of uncertainty. What God has begun in us, His glory will continue to complete.

Night Prayer

God of all creation, my Sovereign King, I thank You for loving me so deeply that You are continually sanctifying and forming me according to Your will and Your way. Even in seasons of uncertainty, guide my steps and steady my heart. Transform my mind so I remember that You are taking me from glory to glory by Your Spirit. Thank You for Your forgiveness, Your unconditional love, and Your amazing grace that sustains me each day. I trust You with the work You are doing in me. In Jesus' name, Amen.

Song of Praise | So Will I - Anthony Evans

Anchoring Reflections
Day 19

1.Where is God inviting me to keep my mind stayed on Him so I can walk in deeper peace?

2. What season of formation am I currently in, and how might God be using it to shape my faith and character?

3. When peace feels distant, what practices help me return my focus to God as my everlasting Rock?

4. How can I surrender more fully to the work God is doing in me, trusting that He is forming me from glory to glory?

Day 20

ANCHORED IN STRENGTH

Anchored in the Morning

Anchoring Scripture

Isaiah 40:31 (KJV)

"But they that wait upon the Lord shall renew their strength; they shall mount up with wings as eagles; they shall run, and not be weary; and they shall walk, and not faint."

Anchoring Thought

With all that Israel went through—and even brought upon themselves—it was still difficult for them to trust that the same God who promised them the Promised Land would continue to forgive them through seasons of disobedience and wavering faith. But God—in His faithfulness and sovereign power—continued to strengthen His people.

God sent prophets to remind Israel of the justice and restoration they would see if they would wait on the Lord, keep walking, and not give up. They were promised that as they waited, they would mount up like eagles—strong, confident, and renewed. Eagles are visionary, strategic, and resilient, and this is the calling placed on us as children of the Most High God.

Anchoring Prayer

Lord, in the fullness of Your grace and the power of Your name, You lift me up. I praise You for Your faithfulness, knowing that You are the same yesterday, today, and forever. I thank You for loving me, fortifying me, and giving me strength for both today and tomorrow. I repent for the times I have relied on my own strength instead of trusting You as the source of all my help. Teach me to wait on You and to draw my strength from Your Spirit. Renew and revive me, God, so that I may rise with strength like an eagle, run and not grow weary, and walk and not faint. I look to You as my anchor in every season and my strength in every storm. In Jesus' name, Amen.

Song of Praise | You Are My Strength - William Murphy

Anchored at Night

Joy in Servitude

Anchoring Scripture

Romans 12:9-13 (NIRV)

"Love must be honest and true. Hate what is evil. Hold on to what is good. Love one another deeply. Honor others more than yourselves. Stay excited about your faith as you serve the Lord. When you hope, be joyful. When you suffer, be patient. When you pray, be faithful. Share with the Lord's people who are in need. Welcome others into your homes."

Anchoring Thought

The Word reminds us that people recognize we belong to God by the way we love. Love is not only what we say—it is how we honor one another, how we show up when it's inconvenient, and how we remain faithful when life is heavy. In Romans, Paul is writing to a community learning what salvation looks like lived out. He teaches that the gospel is not just something we believe; it is something that shapes our character, our relationships, and our daily practices.

Romans 12 calls us into a love that is formed by the Holy Spirit—love that is sincere, steady, and active. Paul urges believers to serve the Lord with spiritual zeal, not as a performance, but as a response to God's mercy. This is why joy, patience in suffering, and devotion to prayer belong together: joy keeps our hearts anchored in hope, patience keeps us steady through trials, and prayer keeps us connected to the Source. When we live this way, our love becomes a living witness of Christ.

This is agape love—the kind of love that gives, serves, forgives, and keeps showing up. It is the love that welcomes, honors, and shares, meeting real needs with real compassion. Romans reminds us that the evidence of God's salvation in us is not only what we confess with our mouths, but how we live with our hands and hearts—loving one another as Christ has loved us.

Night Prayer

Lord my God, when I consider the works of Your hands, my soul is filled with awe. You are great in power, mercy, and glory, and I worship You for who You are. Father, I thank You for being my Lord and Savior and for calling me to serve in Your Kingdom. I offer my life to You as a living sacrifice—holy and pleasing to You. Wherever You have planted my feet, help me to serve faithfully and wholeheartedly for Your glory. Open my eyes to see where You are at work and my heart to obey without fear or wavering. Shape me into a servant leader, fill me with joy for the journey, and let my life reflect the hope found in You. My life belongs to You. In Jesus' name, Amen.

Song of Praise | Give Myself Away / Yes - William McDowell

     DELIA L. MITCHELL

Anchoring Reflections
Day 20

1. Where do I need to wait on the Lord for renewed strength instead of relying on my own effort?

2. What has God been using in this season to strengthen, refine, or form me?

3. How am I currently serving the Lord, and does my service flow from joy or obligation?

4. In what practical ways can I serve others with renewed strength, patience, and faithfulness this week?

Day 21

The Joy of the Cross

Anchored in the Morning

Anchoring Scripture

Hebrews 12:1-3 (NIRV)

"A huge cloud of witnesses is all around us. So let us throw off everything that stands in our way. Let us throw off any sin that holds on to us so tightly. And let us keep on running the race marked out for us. Let us keep looking to Jesus. He is the one who started this journey of faith. And he is the one who completes the journey of faith. He paid no attention to the shame of the cross. He suffered

there because of the joy he was looking forward to. Then he sat down at the right hand of the throne of God. He made it through these attacks by sinners. So think about him. Then you won't get tired. You won't lose hope."

Anchoring Thought

The race is not given to the swift, but to the one who endures to the end. When we think about a race, we understand that preparation matters—conditioning, stretching, nourishment, and consistent practice are necessary to finish well. In the same way, the writer of Hebrews reminds us that our spiritual race requires intention. We are called not only to run, but to lay aside every weight and the sin that so easily entangles us, anything that slows our pace or distracts our focus.

Jesus is our ultimate example. Before He endured the cross, He lived fully in obedience—performing miracles, teaching truth, and preparing His followers for what was ahead. He endured suffering with joy set before Him, showing us how to remain faithful through hardship. As we fix our eyes on Him, we are strengthened to keep running, not growing weary, trusting that endurance produces transformation and leads us to finish the race well.

Anchoring Prayer

God, I come to You with gratitude and worship. I thank You for being the Light of the world and for walking with me through every season. Even in hardship, You remain faithful to Your promises. I thank You for the joy that sustains my soul. I repent for seeking joy outside of You and choose to place my hope in You alone. Help me run my race with my eyes fixed on You, the center of my joy. Create in me a clean heart and renew a right spirit within me. Let the joy You've given overflow to others. In Jesus' name, Amen.

Song of Praise | Everything (Bless The Lord) - Tye Tribbett

Anchored at Night
Anchored in the Word

Anchoring Scripture

Hebrews 4:12 (NIRV)

"The word of God is alive and active. It is sharper than any sword that has two edges. It cuts deep enough to separate soul from spirit. It can separate bones from joints. It judges the thoughts and purposes of the heart."

Anchoring Thought

The Word of God is the living breath of God—alive, active, and powerful. It is the lamp to our feet and the light to our path, guiding us in truth. God's Word reaches deep within us, discerning our thoughts and intentions and aligning our mind, body, and soul with His will. In a world filled with confusion, noise, and shifting truths, we need the Word of God for discernment and for peace. It anchors our hearts and helps us hold on to what is true when everything around us feels uncertain. When we remain anchored in the Word, we are formed, corrected, and sustained by the truth that brings life and stability.

Night Prayer

Heavenly Father, I thank You for Your presence, Your glory, Your holiness, and Your righteousness. I thank You for the gift of the Holy Spirit, who guides, convicts, and comforts me daily.

Lord, I thank You for Your Word. As John 1:1 declares, "In the beginning was the Word, and the Word was with God, and the Word was God." I praise You that Your Word is alive, eternal, and unchanging. Your Word is a lamp to my feet and a light to my path. It gives me discernment, teaches me Your ways, and transforms my heart. Shape me to be anchored, grounded, and equipped because I meditate on Your Word day and night.

Your Word produces obedience, stability, and blessing in my life. It nourishes my soul more than any physical food. Help me to study diligently, live faithfully, and share Your truth boldly with those who are searching. May Your Word dwell richly within me so that everything I do reflects Your love and Your light. In Jesus' name, Amen.

Song of Praise | Evidence - TRIBL, ReFRESH Worship (feat. Naomi Raine)

Anchoring Reflections
Day 21

1. What is God revealing in my heart through His Word that I need to surrender at the Cross?

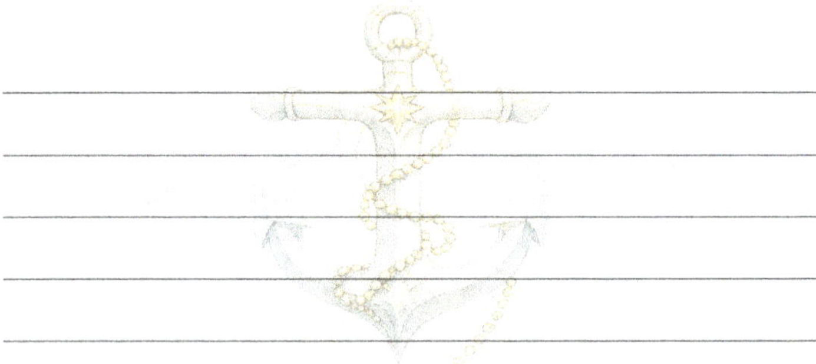

2. How am I allowing the Word of God to shape my thoughts, intentions, and daily choices?

3. Where do I need God's Word to bring me discernment and peace in a world full of noise and shifting truth?

4. How does keeping my eyes on Jesus help me hold on to what is true when life feels uncertain?

5. What intentional step can I take to stay anchored in Scripture so it continues to guide my life?

Week 4: Anchored in Enlightenment

WALKING FORWARD WITH CLARITY AND COURAGE

Day 22

ANCHORED IN POWER

Anchored in the Morning

Anchoring Scripture

Psalm 68:35 (NIRV)

"How wonderful is God in his holy place!
The God of Israel gives power and strength to his people.
Give praise to God!"

Anchoring Thought
Our God is faithful to what He has promised His children. The same God

who led the children of Israel out of bondage and sustained them in every land is the same God who empowers us today—the power He placed on Moses is still alive and at work. We choose to stay grounded in the truth that all power rests in God's hands, and we declare that He does not withhold strength from His children. Therefore, we walk in that power, trusting the one true God, and we give Him all the praise.

Anchoring Prayer

Most holy and wise God, oh how great You are. I thank You for Your presence and for the power You freely give to Your people. Thank You for withholding no good thing and for strengthening us to walk in boldness, freedom, and honor. You have called us not to shrink back, but to live grounded in truth and guided by Your Spirit. Help me use the power You have given me to walk by faith, to live in obedience, and to remain anchored to You in every season. May my life reflect Your glory, and may all I do bring You praise. In Jesus' name, Amen.

Song of Praise | Your Power - Lecrae, Tasha Cobbs Leonard

Anchored at Night
Anchored to Disrupt

Anchoring Scripture

Luke 4:18-19 (NIRV)
"The Spirit of the Lord is on me.
He has anointed me
to announce the good news to poor people.
He has sent me to announce freedom for prisoners.
He has sent me so that the blind will see again.
He wants me to set free those who are treated badly.
And he has sent me to announce the year when he will set his people free."

Anchoring Thought
Anchored in the power of the Spirit, we are called to disrupt anything that leads us away from the truth of God's Word. As Jesus declared freedom, healing, and release in Luke 4:18–19, we are empowered to confront false influence, resist false teaching, and challenge injustice. This disruption is not rooted in pride or anger, but in obedience, love, and a commitment to what reflects the heart of God. When we remain anchored in Christ, we are given the courage to speak truth, expose what is unlike God, and participate in the liberating work of the Kingdom. We disrupt what deceives. We reject what oppresses. We proclaim what restores—because the Spirit of the Lord is upon us.

Night Prayer
Lord of Justice and Lord of Peace,
I give You glory, honor, and my whole heart in worship. I bring before You those carrying grief, neglect, and pain, and I hold before You families harmed by

injustice and systems that divide rather than heal. I trust You as my Deliverer—a God who is both just and merciful. I rest in the truth that no earthly power overrides Your authority. Because I am Your child, I receive the courage to speak truth to power, to disrupt injustice, and to confront anything that is unlike You. Anchor me in obedience and love. Remind me of my responsibility to care for the vulnerable, to do justice, love mercy, and walk humbly with You. Use my voice, my presence, and my life to create healing spaces where hope can rise. Form me—and Your Church—to be bold in love, steadfast in justice, and anchored in truth. In Jesus' name, Amen.

Song of Praise | Anointing - Tobe Nwigwe (feat. Yael Hilton & Ivory Nwigwe)

Anchoring Reflections

Day 22

1.Where am I being invited to receive God's power rather than rely on my own strength?

2. What false belief, influence, or injustice is the Spirit calling me to disrupt or challenge?

3. How can I speak truth in love while remaining anchored in obedience and humility?

____

____

____

____

4. Where is God asking me to use my voice, presence, or position to bring freedom, healing, or hope?

____

____

____

____

Day 23

Anchored in Endurance

Anchored in the Morning

Anchoring Scripture

Exodus 33:14 (NIRV)

"The Lord replied, 'I will go with you. And I will give you rest.'"

Anchoring Thought

The book of Exodus tells the story of the Israelites' departure from Egyptian slavery. Though weary, traumatized, and unsure of what lay ahead, they knew they would have to endure in order to reach the Promised Land. Even when the journey took longer than it should have, God gave them the strength to continue. It was God's presence that brought them rest in the midst of every battle—and it is that same rest He gives us daily as we endure. Even in the waiting, I endure because God's presence goes with me and His rest sustains me.

Anchoring Prayer

Faithful God, I thank You for Your presence that goes with me and Your glory that surrounds me, bringing rest even when the journey feels long. When the way forward is unclear, help me endure without losing my trust in You. Anchor me in Your promises when I grow weary, and remind me that I never walk alone. Teach me to move at Your pace, to rest in Your presence, and to remain faithful in the waiting. Let my endurance reflect Your glory. In Jesus' name, Amen.

Song of Praise | Glorify Your Name - Lakewood Church

Anchored at Night
Anchored in the Garden

Anchoring Scripture

Genesis 2:15 (NIRV)

"The Lord God put the man in the Garden of Eden. He put him there to farm its land and take care of it."

Anchoring Thought

God entrusted humanity with both responsibility and care when He placed us in the Garden. From the beginning, we were called to be intentional stewards of what He placed in our hands. The Garden represents trust, redemption, and compassion—a sacred space where God walks with us, tends to our needs, and invites us into faithful care. Even when we make mistakes, we are not cast out of His presence; we are met with mercy and the opportunity to begin again. Anchored in the Garden, I trust the God who restores what is broken, nurtures what is growing, and gently holds me while teaching me to steward well.

Night Prayer

Dear God of Creation, thank You for Your presence, Your mercy, and the opportunity to begin again. Thank You for Your compassion, even when I do not steward the garden of my mind, body, and spirit well. Walk with me in the places that need tending. Restore what I have neglected, prune what is unhealthy, and nurture what You are growing within me. Help me to care intentionally for what You have entrusted to me, and anchor me in the assurance that I am never outside of Your loving hands. In Jesus' name, Amen.

Song of Praise | In the Garden - Marvin Sapp

Anchoring Reflections

Day 23

1. Where is God inviting me to endure with trust rather than rush the process?

2. What area of my life—mind, body, or spirit—needs more intentional tending and stewardship?

3. How does remembering that God's presence goes with me change the way I face long or uncertain seasons?

4. What might it look like to receive God's mercy and opportunity to begin again instead of dwelling in regret?

Day 24

ANCHORED IN VICTORY

Anchored in the Morning

Anchoring Scripture

1 John 5:4-5 (NIRV)

"That's because everyone who is a child of God has won the battle over the world. Our faith has won the battle for us. Who is it that has won the battle over the world? Only the person who believes that Jesus is the Son of God."

Anchoring Thought

It is easy to believe that victory is a destination—that one day we simply arrive and remain there. But as children born of God, we do not arrive at victory; we walk in it. Scripture reminds us that everyone who is a child of God has already won the battle over the world, and that our faith is what secures that victory (1 John 5:4). Because the One who lives in us is greater than anything in this world (1 John 4:4), our overcoming is not rooted in circumstance, personality, or power—it is rooted in Christ. The resurrection secured what no system, trial, or opposition can undo. Our victory flows from the finished work of the One who conquered sin and the grave. I declare that I do not fight for victory—I stand in the victory already won through Christ. Greater is He who is in me, and nothing in this world has the final word over my life.

Anchoring Prayer

Lord God, by faith through grace we are saved, and we thank You. Thank You that we do not fight for victory, but that in You we already have the victory. Because of Christ, peace is ours, joy is ours, and love is ours. Teach me to live from this truth and not from fear or striving. Let my life reflect the confidence of one who stands in what You have already secured. Anchor my heart in faith, and remind me daily that my victory rests in You. In Jesus' name, Amen.

Song of Praise | Victory Belongs to Jesus - Todd Dulaney

Anchored at Night
New Ground

Anchoring Scripture

Luke 5:36-39 (NIV)
"He told them this parable: 'No one tears a piece out of a new garment to patch an old one. Otherwise, they will have torn the new garment, and the patch from the new will not match the old. And no one pours new wine into old wineskins. Otherwise, the new wine will burst the skins; the wine will run out and the wineskins will be ruined. No, new wine must be poured into new wineskins. And no one after drinking old wine wants the new, for they say, "The old is better."'"

Anchoring Thought
God is awesome in all His ways. He rescued us when we were sinking in sin and loved us enough that we would not perish but have everlasting life in Him. A day in His courts is better than a thousand elsewhere, and we long to enter His presence with thanksgiving and praise.

As we step into new beginnings, we remember that grace calls us forward—not backward. In Luke 5, Jesus reminds us that new wine cannot be poured into old wineskins. Anchored in new ground means putting off the old self and allowing our spirits to be renewed so we can carry what God is pouring. We repent for staying where we should have grown, and we surrender to the new power and freedom He offers. Our lives are in His hands. We receive the new wine. We step onto new ground. We trust the God who restores, renews, and makes all things new.

Night Prayer
Lord, You are the Potter and I am the clay. Shape me according to Your will.

Thank You for rescuing me, restoring me, and calling me into new life. I repent for the times I tried to cling to old ways that could not carry what You are pouring. Mold my heart. Stretch my capacity. Remove what no longer fits the new wine You are releasing in this season. Where I have resisted growth, soften me. Where I have feared change, steady me. As I step onto new ground, form me into a vessel that can steward Your power and freedom well. My life is in Your hands—have Your way in me and make me new. In Jesus' name, Amen.

Song of Praise | New Wine - Hillsong Worship

Anchoring Reflections

Day 24

1.Where do I need to shift from striving for victory to standing in the victory Christ has already secured?

2. What "old wineskin" (mindset, habit, fear, or identity) can no longer carry what God is pouring into my life?

3. How is God stretching my capacity in this season, and where am I resisting growth?

4. What would it look like to step onto new ground with gratitude for grace and readiness for responsibility?

Day 25

ANCHORED IN WISDOM

Anchored in the Morning

Anchoring Scripture

Ecclesiastes 7:12 (NIV)

"Wisdom is a shelter as money is a shelter, but the advantage of knowledge is this: Wisdom preserves those who have it."

Anchoring Thought

Wisdom is more than insight—it is protection. Scripture reminds us that wisdom is a shelter, and unlike temporary security, it preserves those who carry it. Money may guard comfort, but wisdom guards life. Anchored in wisdom means choosing discernment over impulse, patience over reaction, and truth over opinion. It means allowing God's understanding to cover and guide every step. When I seek God's wisdom, I am not merely informed—I am preserved.

Anchoring Prayer

Heavenly Father, what grace You give to me. Thank You for direction and for showing me a way to live that is led by Your wisdom. Thank You for Your patience when I fail to apply what You have already revealed. Thank You for making wisdom accessible to me—simply by asking. You are compassionate and kind, never withholding guidance from those who seek You. Shelter me in Your wisdom. Preserve me through Your understanding. Order my steps so that I walk in ways that honor You and protect what You have entrusted to me. I am grateful for Your steady hand and Your faithful instruction. In Jesus' name, Amen.

Song of Praise | God I Look To You - Tasha Cobbs Leonard

Anchored at Night
Anchored in Discernment

Anchoring Scripture

1 John 4:1-3 (NIRV)

"Dear friends, do not believe every spirit. Test the spirits to see if they belong to God. Many false prophets have gone out into the world. Here is how you can recognize the Spirit of God. Every spirit agreeing that Jesus Christ came in a human body belongs to God. But every spirit that doesn't agree with this does not belong to God. You have heard that the spirit of the great enemy of Christ is coming. Even now it is already in the world."

Anchoring Thought

The words of 1 John remain deeply relevant in every generation. What was present then is still present now—voices that sound convincing yet do not align with Christ. Scripture warns us not to believe every spirit, but to test what we hear to see whether it truly belongs to God. As followers of Christ, this is not optional—it is necessary.

Discernment is a gift from God, and it grows through time spent in His presence. The only way to test a spirit is to know the Word of God. His Word corrects, edifies, and encourages—it is His very breath. Without studying Scripture for ourselves and seeking God in prayer, we risk being tossed to and fro, carried by every new doctrine or persuasive voice.

Anchored in wisdom means holding fast to the true and living God and allowing His Word to be the measure by which all things are tested. When we remain grounded in Him, we are not easily deceived—we are steady, rooted, and preserved.

Night Prayer

Heavenly Father, thank You for the gift of Your Word and the guidance of Your Spirit. Teach me not to believe everything I hear, but to test what comes before me according to the truth of Christ. Guard my heart from deception and anchor my mind in what is true. Increase my hunger for Scripture. Help me to study Your Word for myself so that I may recognize Your voice above all others. When persuasive voices rise around me, steady me in discernment. Keep me from being tossed by every doctrine or distracted by what does not reflect You. Form in me a wisdom that comes from time spent in Your presence. Let Your Word correct me, edify me, and strengthen me. I choose to hold fast to the true and living God. Preserve me through Your truth, and let my life reflect clarity, conviction, and faithfulness. In Jesus' name, Amen.

Song of Praise | Be Still and Know - CeCe Winans

Anchoring Reflections

Day 25

1. What voices, influences, or ideas am I allowing to shape my thinking—and do they align with the truth of God's Word?

2. Where do I need to ask God for wisdom instead of reacting from emotion, impulse, or assumption?

3. How consistent am I in studying Scripture for myself so that I can recognize what is truly from God?

____

____

____

____

____

4. What practical step can I take this week to strengthen my spiritual discernment and protect what God has entrusted to me?

____

____

____

____

____

Day 26

New Life in the Spirit

Anchored in the Morning

Anchoring Scripture

John 6:63 (NKJV)

"It is the Spirit who gives life; the flesh profits nothing. The words that I speak to you are spirit, and they are life."

Anchoring Thought

"The Spirit gives life." These words are victory in themselves—a steady reminder that true life does not come from the flesh, performance, or public approval, but from God alone. When Jesus spoke these words, many turned away because the teaching was difficult. Yet the truth did not change: it is the Spirit who gives life.

When we accepted Him, we received more than forgiveness—we received new life. This life is our freedom. It assures us that sin no longer has the final hold over us. When we repent and turn toward Him, we are not left in bondage. The Holy Spirit renews us daily, breathing strength, clarity, and hope into places that once felt confined. Even if others walk away, the Spirit still gives life. Anchored in Him, I live from freedom, not fear, sustained by the breath of God that restores me each day.

Anchoring Prayer

Lord Jesus, You said that the Spirit gives life, and today I choose to believe that truth. Forgive me for the times I have been tempted to turn away when Your teaching felt difficult. Forgive me for following the crowd instead of following You, for seeking comfort over conviction, and approval over obedience. When others walk away, anchor my heart in Your Word. Give me courage to remain when the path is narrow and steady faith when truth is unpopular. I repent of drifting toward what feels easy instead of staying rooted in the One who gives life. Holy Spirit, breathe on me again. Renew my commitment. Restore my focus. Let me not be swayed by voices that pull me from You. Keep me grounded in repentance, covered in grace, and alive in Your presence. I do not want to follow the crowd—I want to follow Christ. In Jesus' name, Amen.

Song of Praise | My Soul Follows - David & Nicole Binion (feat. Travis Greene)

Anchored at Night
Fullness of Life

Anchoring Scripture

Ezekiel 37:13-14 (NIRV)

"So I will open up your graves and bring you out of them. Then you will know that I am the Lord. You are my people. I will put my Spirit in you. And you will live again. I will settle you in your own land. Then you will know that I have spoken. I have done it,' announces the Lord."

Anchoring Thought

In Ezekiel 37, God declares that He will open graves, bring His people out, put His Spirit within them, and they will live again. This promise reminds us that fullness of life is not found in this world as our final destination. There will be valley seasons—dry places, dark places, moments that feel buried. Yet the Lord speaks resurrection over what appears finished.

Fullness is not the absence of valleys; it is the presence of the Spirit within them. Even in dark places, we are not abandoned. Christ, our Rose of Sharon and Lily of the Valley, meets us there. These biblical images from Song of Songs symbolize His beauty, purity, and faithful love—reminding us that hope can bloom even in harsh places and that God's presence is tender yet strong in the valley. Our life becomes full not by pursuing status, security, or striving, but by trusting God's Word, resting in His Spirit, and being still enough to know that He has spoken—and He will do it. Anchored in Christ, I trust the God who brings life out of graves and fullness out of what once felt empty.

Night Prayer

Faithful God, You are the One who opens graves and calls dry places back to life. Thank You for putting Your Spirit within me and breathing life where I once felt empty. When I find myself in valley seasons, remind me that the valley is not the end of my story. Lord, teach me that fullness is found in You—not in striving, comparison, or chasing what fades. In dark places, be my Lily of the Valley. In dry seasons, be my Rose of Sharon. Let Your beauty, purity, and faithful love bloom in the very places I thought were barren. Help me trust that what You have spoken, You will accomplish. Anchor me in stillness. Anchor me in hope. Anchor me in the assurance that Your Spirit sustains me and that my life is full because You are near. I rest in the fullness that comes from Your presence alone. In Jesus' name, Amen.

Song of Praise | Nothing Like Your Presence - William McDowell (feat. Travis Greene & Nathaniel Bassey)

Anchoring Reflections

Day 26

1. Where in my life do I need the Holy Spirit to breathe new life into something that feels dry, tired, or buried?

2. Have I been seeking fullness through striving or comparison instead of trusting in Christ's presence?

3. In what ways have I been tempted to "turn away" from truth when it feels difficult, and how can I remain anchored in the Spirit?

____

4. What valley season in my life could become a place where God's beauty and hope bloom instead of defeat?

____

Day 27

ANCHORED. WHERE I STARTED. WHERE I AM.

Anchored in the Morning

Anchoring Thought

Growth is rarely loud. It happens in obedience, surrender, correction, endurance, and renewal. What once felt fragile may now feel rooted. What once felt uncertain may now carry clarity. Pausing is not regression—it is recognition. Reflection allows us to see the faithfulness of God and the quiet formation within ourselves. Anchored living is not perfection; it is progression in Christ.

Although these 28 days are coming to an end, this companion was never meant to replace your walk with God—it was meant to walk beside you. It is simply a reminder, a steady voice pointing you back to light, obedience, and truth. The journey does not stop here. You continue forward, letting God's Word shape you and prayer sustain you. Anchored living is not a 28-day practice; it is a lifelong posture of trusting the One who guides your steps.

Anchoring Prayer

Faithful God, thank You for the growth You have formed in me—seen and unseen. Thank You for walking with me through peace and joy, discipline and community, power and endurance, wisdom and renewal. As I pause to reflect, I recognize that every step has been guided by Your hand. Though these 28 days come to a close, my walk with You continues. Anchor me in light, obedience, and truth. Let Your Word remain my foundation and prayer remain my breath. Guard me from returning to old patterns, and strengthen my desire to live anchored in You. Remind me that this journey is not about completing pages but about cultivating presence. Shape me daily. Correct me gently. Lead me faithfully. I choose to continue walking in what You have begun. My life is Yours. Keep me anchored. In Jesus' name, Amen.

Song of Praise | I Thank God - TRIBL (feat. Maverick City Music & UPPERROOM)

Anchored at Night

Rest Here.

This evening is yours — no structure, no prompt, no expectation. Simply be with God. Let the last 27 days settle. Tomorrow, we finish.

No Scripture. No prayer. Just presence.

Anchoring Reflections

Day 27

I honor the growth I cannot always see. I trust the formation God is doing within me. I remain anchored.

1.Growth

When I compare Day 1 to today, where have I grown spiritually—quietly but clearly?

2. Formation

Which anchor (peace, joy, discipline, community, power, endurance, wisdom, new life) has formed me the most?

3. Surrender

Where am I still resisting surrender?

4. Teaching

What has God consistently been teaching me across these days?

5. Faithfulness

How do I see evidence of God's faithfulness in my life since beginning this journey?

Day 28

ANCHORED IN THE WEEDS & MARVELOUS THINGS

There is something sacred about finishing what once felt overwhelming.

When you began this 28-day journey, you were not trying to be impressive. You were trying to be anchored. Somewhere between peace and discipline, between endurance and new ground, something shifted. You stopped writing about anchoring—and started living it more intentionally.

The weeds were real.
The doubts were real.
The stretching was real.
But so was the grace.

Being anchored in the weeds means understanding that growth does not always look polished. It looks like quiet obedience. It looks like repentance that no one applauds. It looks like choosing wisdom when emotion would be easier. It looks like staying when walking away would be simpler.

And yet—marvelous things happened there.

The Lord did not wait for the garden to be tidy before He moved. He moved in the weeds. He formed you in places no one else could see. He deepened your roots when you felt buried. What once felt like resistance became refinement. What felt like delay became direction.

Marvelous things are not always loud miracles. Sometimes they are subtle transformations—clarity replacing confusion, peace silencing panic, courage rising where fear once lived.

That is the marvel.

You are not ending this journey as the person who started it.

And even though these 28 days close, anchored living continues. This companion was never meant to be your source. It was meant to point you back to the true Source. You will still wake up needing peace. You will still choose joy. You will still practice discipline. You will still lean into community. You will still disrupt, endure, discern, and trust the Spirit.

But now you know something you didn't fully know before:
God works in the weeds.
And He does marvelous things there.

Stay anchored.
Stay humble.
Stay rooted in His Word and steady in prayer.

The journey was not about completion.
It was about formation. And formation continues.

With gratitude for the weeds,
and awe for the marvelous things!

Night Prayer

Lord, thank You for every weed. Thank You for every marvelous thing.
I came to this journey uncertain. I leave it more rooted than I arrived.
You were faithful in the quiet. You were faithful in the hard.
Keep me anchored — not just for 28 days, but for every day that follows.
My life is Yours. In Jesus' name, Amen.

Song of Praise | Firm Foundation (He Won't) - Cody Carnes / Maverick City Music

A Year
of Anchored
Living

REPEATED. DEEPENED. REFINED.

This is **not just a 28-day rhythm** — it is a yearly cycle of **anchored forma-tion.**

Return to it.

Revisit it.

Live it.

Peace — Resting in the faithfulness of God.
Scriptures: Isaiah 26:3-4 · Psalm 91:1-2 · John 14:27

Joy — Rooted gladness beyond circumstance.
Scriptures: 1 Peter 1:8-9 · Zephaniah 3:17 · Nehemiah 8:10

Discipline — Formed through obedience and surrender.
Scriptures: Proverbs 16:3 · Hebrews 12:11 · 2 Corinthians 3:18

Community — Strengthened together, never alone.
Scriptures: Ecclesiastes 4:9-10 · Acts 2:42 · Galatians 6:2

Power — Walking in the authority God freely gives.
Scriptures: Psalm 68:35 · Luke 4:18-19 · 2 Timothy 1:7

Endurance — Holding on when the journey grows long.
Scriptures: Exodus 33:14 · Hebrews 12:1-3 · Romans 5:3-4

Wisdom — Discerning truth and walking preserved.
Scriptures: Ecclesiastes 7:12 · 1 John 4:1-3 · James 1:5

New Life — Trusting the Spirit to breathe again.
Scriptures: John 6:63 · Ezekiel 37:13-14 · 2 Corinthians 5:17

Anchored in the Sound

A Companion Playlist (Scan QR code)

This journey was never meant to be read in silence.

Throughout these pages, there were moments of peace, wrestling, joy, surrender, courage, repentance, and renewal. Music has a way of carrying what words sometimes cannot. It helps truth settle. It helps prayer rise. It helps the Spirit move.

This curated playlist was created to accompany your anchoring journey.

Listen:
- In the morning before you begin your day
- During quiet reflection
- While journaling
- When you need to remember what God has spoken
- When the weeds feel heavy and you need to hear hope again

Let these songs remind you of:

Peace that guards.

Joy that strengthens.

Discipline that forms.

Community that surrounds.

Victory that stands.

Wisdom that preserves.

Life that breathes again.

About the author

Delia Mitchell is first a mother—raising two daughters who daily remind her why faith must be lived and not just spoken. A native of Louisville, Kentucky, she carries the strength of her roots and the tenderness of her upbringing into every space she serves.

She is a minister of the Gospel whose calling has been shaped as much in quiet prayer closets as in classrooms. A proud graduate of Kentucky State University, Delia later completed theological studies at Colgate Rochester Crozer Divinity School, where she continues pursuing her Master of Divinity. Her faith has been formed through Scripture, surrender, stretching, and seasons that required her to stay anchored when life felt overgrown.

As a Certified Life Coach and founder of Honor Your Vision Life Coaching, LLC, and as a Certified Biblical Counselor, she walks alongside others navigating their own "weeds" — helping them grow deep roots rather than quick fixes.

Delia writes the way she lives: anchored in truth, honest about growth, and expectant of God's work in ordinary places. This book was not written from perfection, but from progression.

She believes God still forms people in quiet places—and she is living proof.

Still learning. Still growing. Still anchored.
~ Delia